JOHN ERIK FOSSUM
HANS PETTER GRAV

SQUARING THE CIRCLE ON BREXIT

Could the Norway model work?

BRISTOL
UNIVERSITY
PRESS

First published in Great Britain in 2018 by

Bristol University Press
University of Bristol
1-9 Old Park Hill
Bristol
BS2 8BB
UK
t: +44 (0)117 954 5940
www.bristoluniversitypress.co.uk

North America office:
Bristol University Press
c/o The University of Chicago Press
1427 East 60th Street
Chicago, IL 60637, USA
t: +1 773 702 7700
f: +1 773 702 9756
sales@press.uchicago.edu
www.press.uchicago.edu

© Bristol University Press 2018

British Library Cataloguing in Publication Data
A catalogue record for this book is available from the British Library.

Library of Congress Cataloging-in-Publication Data
A catalog record for this book has been requested.

ISBN 978-1-5292-0030-0 (paperback)
ISBN 978-1-5292-0032-4 (ePub)
ISBN 978-1-5292-0033-1 (Mobi)
ISBN 978-1-5292-0031-7 (ePDF)

The right of John Erik Fossum and Hans Petter Graver to be identified as authors of this work
has been asserted by them in accordance with the Copyright, Designs and Patents Act 1988.

Cover design by blu inc, Bristol
Front cover: image kindly supplied by Stocksy
Printed and bound in Great Britain by CMP, Poole
Bristol University Press uses environmentally responsible print partners

Contents

Foreword

Interest in Norway's relations with the European Union has intensified since the British referendum in June 2016 and the Brexit process now under way. This book is a timely and welcome contribution to the British and wider European debates.

The European Union has negotiated many agreements with European countries seeking a relationship with it, but unwilling or unprepared to join it. The solution for Norway was found in the European Economic Area which that country shares with Iceland, Liechtenstein and the EU countries.

It is for Norwegians to judge whether the 'Norway model' works for them. The British Government has rejected all existing models and seeks something new and unprecedented. The metaphor of choice is 'bespoke'. Only the outcome of the negotiations will tell us what this means in practice. It is likely to involve compromise and accommodation. In the EEA (and Schengen), Norway is integrated into the EU's single market regulatory system with a different institutional framework, but is generally perceived to be a 'rule-taker' with only limited influence over the making of the rules it takes and applies.

There are complex realities on both sides of the relationship between the United Kingdom and the European Union. The United Kingdom, to adapt the geometrical metaphor of the book's title, combines a triangular island, Great Britain, with part of the neighbouring island of Ireland. As George Orwell pointed out in 1941: 'we call our islands by no less than six different names, England, Britain, Great Britain, the British Isles, the United Kingdom and, in very exalted moments, Albion'. The list is a bit outdated, but the point was well made. The United Kingdom is oddly shaped constitutionally. The EU meanwhile is made up of 27 countries, excluding the UK, some of which participate in all of its activities, while others do not. The continent of Europe in the traditional understanding of its geography contains states big and small, UN Security Council members, neutral countries, islands and landlocked states, former colonies, former colonial powers, countries which recently shook off dictatorships, were occupied or occupied others, and so on. The UK is unique in leaving the Union after 45 years as a member, and, while rejecting the various arrangements in place for non-Union countries, has so far been unable or unwilling to articulate a blueprint for its future relationship. That blueprint will emerge from democratic debate within the UK and negotiations with the EU, itself channeling the democratic politics of the 27 remaining member states through the institutions of the Union. The Norway model will be close to the forefront of people's minds as various shapes are remodelled into something new and different. It is therefore important to understand how Norway experiences its European relationships and interacts with the states and institutions of the European Union.

Sir Jonathan Faull KCMG,
Visiting Professor Vrije Universiteit Brussel, King's College
London, College of Europe;
Chair, European Public Affairs, Brunswick Group;
European Commission 1978-2016.

Preface and acknowledgements

To most citizens and analysts alike, the UK referendum decision on 23 June 2016 to leave the European Union came as a shock. And even if the UK referendum debate was rather introverted, the Brexit decision has given rise to a broad debate not only in the UK but across Europe. It still remains unclear what future relationship the UK will have with the rest of Europe. Provided Brexit ensues, it has become ever more apparent that the effects will be significant. We in Norway have suddenly discovered that our relationship with the EU through the EEA Agreement and a host of other arrangements has entered centre stage in the UK debate, epitomised by the so-called Norway model. This form of association is lauded and dismissed as a possible solution for the UK. There is, however, no discussion of the implications for Norway and the other EEA states of the UK adopting this model, even if the effects on these states will be very significant. In this book we provide an overview of the Norway model, and an assessment of the likelihood that the UK will adopt (parts of or all of) this model. As part of that we discern some lessons from Norway's experience with this type of EU affiliation, a brief discussion of the transferability of these lessons to the UK, and some reflections on the possible effects on Norway. The book combines law and politics and their vantage points for analysing the complex and composite nature of the phenomena involved. As we were preparing the book, Rosa Greaves organised a seminar in Glasgow which enabled us to discuss some of the ideas and findings of the book with a range of experts. We are very grateful for this. We are also grateful for comments and suggestions on the entire manuscript from Chris Lord, an anonymous reader at Bristol University Press and the proposal reviewers. We would like to thank our institutions at the University of Oslo for support, especially ARENA for excellent editorial assistance by Ragnhild Grønning and Jorunn Kristina Skodje. We also thank the Institute of Advanced Study at Durham University which generously hosted Graver for the university term following the Brexit vote. Finally, we are very grateful to Stephen Wenham at BUP for his enthusiastic support.

List of abbreviations

CBI	Confederation of British Industry
CETA	Comprehensive Economic and Trade Agreement
CJEU	Court of Justice of the European Union
ECA	European Communities Act 1972
ECHR	European Court of Human Rights
ECJ	European Court of Justice
EDA	European Defence Agency
EEA	European Economic Area
EFTA	European Free Trade Association
ESA	EFTA Surveillance Authority
JMC	Joint Ministerial Committees
NATO	North Atlantic Treaty Organization
NHO	Norwegian Business Association
OSCE	Organisation of Security and Cooperation
PESCO	Permanent Structured Cooperation
SCA	Surveillance and Court Agreement
SIS	Schengen Information System
TEU	Treaty on European Union
TFEU	Treaty on the Functioning of the European Union
TUC	Trade Union Congress
WEAG	Western European Armament Group
WTO	World Trade Organization

Introduction

After seven decades of integration of Europe, cracks are appearing. The United Kingdom's decision to leave the European Union after the negative referendum result on 23 June 2016 is the most dramatic instance thus far of rejecting the EU's credo of 'ever closer union'. There have been membership referendum rejections in the periphery of Europe (Norway 1972 and 1995, Switzerland 1994), and treaty and other referendum rejections within the EU itself.[1] Nevertheless, the decision of a major member state to exit the Union is unprecedented. Brexit (combined with the EU's other crises) has prompted reflection and debate on the EU's further development. At the same time, and especially for an entity that Jacques Delors has depicted as a UPO or unidentified political object,[2] the way it handles the loss of a major member offers important insights into the system's self-conception. What is apparent from the manner in which the EU has handled the process of Brexit thus far is that it sees itself as a legal and political entity, and even if it is not a state, it has elements of stateness and responds to such momentous developments in a state-like manner. At the same time its functions and scope of action are defined by treaties that give wide powers to the Court of Justice to define and limit the action of the institutions and the member states. As we shall see, that clearly shapes the process and what the EU is prepared to offer to the UK.

The UK's decision to exit the EU will situate it in a new category of state in Europe: that of ex-member state (Lord, 2015). Once the UK leaves the EU, almost regardless of the shape of its future relationship to the rest of Europe, it will be part of a heterogeneous group of states that are *associated* with the EU, as the UK will most likely have *some form of association* with the EU post-Brexit. It is therefore useful to search for possible analogies in order to see if they hold relevant lessons for the UK.

The states that are not members of the EU but instead have some form of association with it vary greatly with regard to the range and density of association, and in terms of whether or not they qualify for EU membership (Gstöhl, 2015). The UK, in its effort to smooth the transition from EU member to non-member has on the one hand announced that it will incorporate (most of) EU law into UK law through the European Union Withdrawal Bill, and on the other hand is likely to settle a transition arrangement with the EU of roughly two years' duration. The point is to avoid a cliff-edge when the UK formally leaves the EU, which would be at midnight on 29 March 2019.

When considering where to locate the UK within the group of affiliated EU non-members, it is obvious (for numerous reasons not least relating to the specifics of the states involved) that the UK will most closely resemble those states that qualify for EU membership, but do not want to become EU members. Only a handful of the associated states, or more specifically the European Free Trade Association (EFTA) members – Switzerland, Norway, Iceland and Lichtenstein, where the latter three make up the European Economic Area (EEA) Agreement – qualify for EU membership, which is a condition for assured access to the EU's internal market. It is to this group of states that the UK will belong after Brexit, and it is this group of states that provides the most relevant experiences for the UK post-Brexit.

The main purpose of this book is to contribute to the UK debate with an in-depth assessment of the type of affiliation that Norway has developed with the EU. Norway is by far the largest EFTA member of the EEA, and it is the one that is most frequently discussed in the UK in connection with Brexit, hence the notion of the 'Norway model'. The model is similar to those of Iceland and Liechtenstein, and could therefore be referred to as the 'EFTA model' or the 'EEA model'. But the affiliation goes beyond the EEA Agreement, and each EFTA country has its own type of association with the EU, and its own interests and reasons for it. A further ground for focusing on Norway is that it is the only EEA member that has rejected EU membership in a popular referendum, and has actually done so twice, in 1972 and 1994. The analogy with Brexit extends further in the sense that Norway had entered into the EEA Agreement with the EU (the agreement entered into force on 1 January 1994) *before* the popular referendum that rejected Norwegian EU membership (28 November 1994). Both the UK and Norway had therefore adopted a broad body of EU rules and norms *before* the referenda that rejected EU membership. Thus, even if the subsequent developments proceed in different directions: for Norway it is about increased EU incorporation (so much so that many have said that the no-sayers won on the day of the referendum, 28 November 1994, yet have lost every day since), whereas for the UK it is about dismantling its EU affiliation, both need to contend with the EU rules and norms that so extensively programme their legal and political systems and societies. In effect, all affiliated states, and in particular the closely affiliated ones (which enjoy assured access to the EU's internal market), face a trilemma in their relations with the EU, which refers to the need for *balancing effective external governance* (ability to influence externally generated rules and norms); *assured market access*; and *popular support and legitimacy* (Featherstone, 2017, 1; with reference to Rodrik, 2011).

Our assessment of 'the Norway model' and the possible lessons it might yield for the UK combines legal and political perspectives and explicitly addresses the trilemma. We combine legal and political perspectives for the simple fact that the actors have different expectations of the process. Put simply, the UK government seeks a range of bespoke agreements and underlines the need for bargaining, and hence places the stress on politics, whereas the EU is particularly concerned with developing procedures and guidelines for how the process may proceed and would prefer to offer the UK an off-the-shelf solution, with the Norway model as a frequent reference. The EU thus seeks to juridify the Brexit issue, and to close down the scope for politics and political bargaining. At the end of the day, the Court of Justice will have the final say, both on whether the EU–UK deal is compatible with the EU treaties, and on whether it succeeds in obtaining the type of association that the parties aim for. We thus see actors with different expectations of the process and its outcome. The December 2017 Withdrawal Agreement suggests that the EU's approach has won out thus far.

In order to try to discern lessons from Norway as part of the discussion on whether the Norway model might work for the UK, we need to know what type of EU affiliation the UK seeks, and how it compares with Norway's. That, of course, presupposes clarifying the type of EU affiliation that the Norway model entails, not only in terms of how Norway's EU relationship is structured but also in terms of how this affiliation is handled domestically in Norway, and the effects it has had on Norway's political and legal system during its 23 years' existence. Based on these examinations, we discern lessons from Norway for the UK, including how transferable they are to the UK. Our discussion of lessons is not confined to those features that characterise Norway as such. Rather, we are concerned with spelling out the features of Norway's experience that, on the one hand, matter most and, on the other hand, are most readily generalisable to the UK context. Finally, we consider the possible implications that this type of UK–EU association could have on Norway, a theme that has thus far not entered the UK debate.

We are concerned with crafting the book in such a manner that its relevance does not hinge on whether the UK opts for the EEA Agreement or not. We cast the net wider and include the entire range of Norway's EU affiliation, including informal arrangements. In addition, we have devised the book in such a manner as to ensure as far as possible that the issues we address are relevant to the UK, almost regardless of the type of solution it ends up with.

What this book is about

Chapter One focuses on the UK's objectives, options and constraints in relation to Brexit. The purpose of the chapter is threefold. First, the aim is to establish how the most relevant UK actors envisage their future EU relationship with emphasis on the role and salience that they attribute to the EEA. In order to do so, we will develop a typology of how the Norwegian option has been discussed, and check which option (or options) predominates in the UK debate. The assessment includes how the UK envisages its future EU relationship along the lines of the sum total of arrangements that Norway has with the EU, in order to get a comprehensive picture. That is necessary in terms of the lessons that we may discern from Norway for the UK. We consider the position of the UK government as well as those UK actors (the political parties; nations: the Scottish government's view, that of Wales and that of Northern Ireland; and business and labour unions) that are most likely to be able to influence the nature and shape of the UK position on Brexit. Second, we pay attention to the European Union Withdrawal Bill, which is paradoxically about sustaining a strong EU influence on the UK. Third, we briefly consider what key EU actors prefer, which is important in terms of the room for manoeuvre the UK has.

Chapter Two presents a brief overview of the EU's range of affiliations with non-members. The chapter starts by discussing the EU's distinct approach to borders and bordering, which is clearly of relevance for the UK government's focus on bespoke agreements. The EU is adaptive to its surroundings but has established a set of guidelines and frameworks that shape how it fashions its external relations. We need to pay attention to the EU's principles and guidelines in order to get a handle on the wiggle-room that is available for non-members. Second, the chapter provides a brief overview of the sheer range of off-the-shelf modes of affiliation already out there. Finally, we zoom in on and provide a brief overview of the Swiss model. This chapter thus helps to conceptualise the discussion of the Norway model as one among a broad range of modes of affiliation.

Chapter Three provides an overview of the Norway model, which can be described as EEA++. The chapter is divided into two main parts, where the first focuses on the EEA Agreement, and the second on the other portions of Norway's affiliation with the EU. The first part starts with a brief account of why the EEA Agreement (which encompasses the three EFTA countries and all the EU member states) came about, and what its main objectives were. Thereafter, we provide an overview of the substantive contents of the EEA Agreement, and the main institutions involved. The second part of the chapter focuses on those portions of Norway's EU affiliation that are not included in the EEA Agreement. We focus on the legal and political opportunities and constraints built into the various agreements: EEA, Schengen, Dublin I, II, III. It is interesting to note that some of these arrangements involve Norway more closely with the EU than is the case with the UK. A telling example is the fact that Norway is affiliated with Schengen and therefore is inside the EU's external border with responsibility for EU border protection, whereas the UK is not.

Chapter Four focuses on the elusive concept of sovereignty, and provides a legal reading of sovereignty in relation to the Norway model. We complement this legal analysis with political analysis in the next chapter. In this chapter, we distinguish between legislative, judicial and executive sovereignty. Legislative sovereignty is challenged when an organ outside of the state is empowered to legislate with effect within the state, such as when the EU has the power to enact regulations that are binding in their entirety and are directly applicable in all European Union countries (Article 288 TFEU: Official Journal of the European Union, 2012). Judicial sovereignty is challenged when an external court such as the Court of Justice of the European Union (CJEU) gives rulings that are binding for national courts in dealing with specific cases. Executive sovereignty is challenged when an external body such as the Commission passes decisions that are binding on legal subjects within the state, as they do in competition cases. For these reasons, EU law goes beyond international law and is characterised as supranational.

Chapter Five seeks to discern possible lessons from Norway's EU experience for the UK post-Brexit. In this chapter, we examine the main lessons from Norway's EU experience and discuss how transferable they are to the UK. In the last part of the chapter, we ask how and in what sense the lessons that we have discerned from Norway's experience can be generalised by focusing on the main issues at stake. A central feature of the EEA Agreement is the concept of dynamic homogeneity. Homogeneity means an economic area based on common rules and equal conditions of competition, and providing for the equivalent means of enforcement, including at the judicial level. Because it is dynamic, the homogeneity is also maintained when rules and interpretation of rules change in the EU. In other words, when exploring market access, we discuss how confining dynamic homogeneity is and what scope there might be within such an arrangement for some element of sovereign control and democratic accountability. Conversely, when looking at access to decisions, we consider what scope there might be for wielding influence and to what extent we should expect the UK to be in a qualitatively different position from Norway on that count.

Chapter Six assesses the possible implications of Brexit for the EEA countries. In this chapter, we outline the relevant options that have been discussed thus far for the UK's post-Brexit EU association, and assess the possible implications for the EEA countries, with particular emphasis on Norway. The EU's affiliated countries are not involved in the Brexit negotiations but are kept informed of the developments. It is readily apparent that the outcome of the negotiations will be critically important for them. Thus, we need to assess implications with reference to the triangular relationship: EU-UK-EEA countries. We outline and discuss the following four scenarios: (a) no EU-UK association agreement; (b) UK association agreement with the EU *outside* the context of the EEA; (c) UK association agreement with the EU *within* the context of the EEA; and (d) a two-tiered EU with the UK in the outer tier.

In the concluding chapter, we briefly sum up the main findings and arguments of the book. Particular emphasis is placed on providing a summary assessment of the most likely manner in which the UK will relate to the Norway model.

1

What does Britain want from Brexit?

This chapter focuses on the UK's objectives in relation to Brexit, with emphasis on the role and salience attributed to the Norway model. The post-referendum UK government has quite consistently rejected a future UK-EEA membership as part of its rejection of all off-the-shelf agreements (a relationship that the EU already has with at least one non-member state and which can be extended to include the UK), and has instead stressed the need for a set of bespoke agreements with the EU (a set of agreements that are specially designed for the UK). Views across the UK differ widely on the preferred form of the UK's future EU association, and the government has been widely criticised for lack of clarity and realism. The government's position has then also shifted considerably over time. The 8 December 2017 Withdrawal Agreement shows how it has conceded to the EU on substantive issues and on control of the process. It now acknowledges that there is a need for a period of transition. Close to a year after the negotiations began, it remains unclear what the UK government wants and what it will settle for.

In order to untangle this, we need to consider: (a) the type of future EU association the UK government expresses a commitment to (whatever the details may be), and how it has evolved; (b) those actors and forces that influence this, what they want and how influential they are; (c) who controls the Brexit process (if anyone); and (d) the broader (European and global) context within which this process is unfolding. The unfolding of the Brexit saga thus far suggests that the UK's future relationship with the EU will be determined not by goal-driven government action, but by a complex and unwieldly process that is influenced by a broad range of actors and factors.

The chapter is divided into two main sections. In the first, we consider the position of the UK government, which asserted that 'Brexit means Brexit' in line with the Leave camp's focus on the need for taking back control. In the second section, we consider how this objective is to be carried out by paying attention to those UK actors that are most capable of influencing the course of action. Our survey includes parliament and political parties; devolved nations (the Scottish government's view, that of Wales and that of Northern Ireland); business; and labour unions. Further, we focus on another important aspect of the UK government's position on Brexit, namely:

> That the UK exits the EU with **certainty, continuity and control**. The [European Union (Withdrawal)] Bill ensures that, so far as possible, the same rules and laws will apply on the day after exit as on the day before. This will provide the maximum possible **certainty and continuity** to businesses, workers and consumers across the UK – so that they can have confidence that they will not be subject to unexpected changes on the day we leave the EU. (UK Government, 2017a, 1; emphasis in original)

The Withdrawal Bill is intended to avoid a disruptive cliff-edge. Can disruption and uncertainty be allayed by incorporating *existing* EU laws and regulations or does not the very notion of certainty presuppose a procedure ensuring *future* dynamic homogeneity with EU laws and regulations? The Withdrawal

Agreement provides a preliminary answer, but since David Davis has underlined that 'nothing is agreed until everything is agreed' (European Commission, 2017a, pt. 5), even the fate of the agreement hinges on subsequent developments. The second stage of negotiations is due to start in March 2018. By then the European Council will have formulated a set of guidelines for the future EU–UK agreement (European Council, 2017), and the UK government will spell out its position in further detail.

The UK government's objectives reflect its attempts to balance or reconcile sovereign control with legally regulated access to the EU for the UK (citizens and businesses). This is not something that the UK can determine; whatever balance is struck is worked out by the various portions of the UK and the various portions of the EU *jointly*. We therefore pay attention to what key EU actors prefer, including a brief assessment of how much of the terms of the future relationship they are likely to determine.

In the final concluding part of the chapter, we assess the extent to which the UK has adopted elements of the Norway model, paying heed to the following options: (i) outright dismissal; (ii) outright embrace; (iii) Norwegian option à la carte/pick-and-mix; (iv) Norwegian option plus; (v) Norwegian option minus; (vi) disguised adoption of the Norwegian option (plus, minus or whatever) while pretending to do something completely different.

An important purpose of the chapter is to show that the 'Norway model' involves a far broader range of EU associations than are covered by the EEA Agreement. We therefore describe the Norway model not as being akin to the EEA Agreement, as depicted in the UK debate, but as *the sum total of a range of modes of association* that differ in terms of institutional arrangements, extent of supranational imprint, and EU enforcement. The sheer range of modes of association in play suggests that even if the UK does not end up in the EEA, it might still adopt elements of the 'Norway model'.

UK objectives

The UK in-out referendum on 23 June 2016 was, formally speaking, advisory. However, most actors are treating it as binding. The question that continues to linger is: *binding in terms of what option to go for?* The binary yes-no referendum choice was not suitable for instructing politicians on the specific option that they should choose from among a range of alternatives on the exit side.[3] In a comprehensive report issued prior to the vote, the government presented three main alternatives to continued EU membership: the Norway model, bilateral negotiated agreements and a World Trade Organization (WTO)-only model (UK Government, 2016), and pointed to the strengths and weaknesses of all three.

Citizens' voting intent does not translate well to the type of future EU relationship that the UK will opt for. That is not unique to the UK, but was also apparent in the Norwegian 1994 EU referendum. When Norway held the referendum on 28 November 1994, the EEA Agreement had come into effect. Hence, with regard to voting intent (not outcome), it was clear what a Yes vote signified, but not whether a No vote signified rejection of EU membership but not the EEA, or whether it entailed rejection of both (Fossum, 2016).

When (lukewarm Remainer) Theresa May became Prime Minister after the referendum, she underlined that 'Brexit means Brexit'. However, there was no plan B; the referendum did not establish a clear set of instructions for what type of relationship the UK would have with the EU post-Brexit; and the government faced a severe lack of administrative and technical expertise, in particular negotiating expertise (Parker and Pickard, 2017).[4] In addition, the government was stacked with ministers with different views on what type of future EU relationship the UK should opt for. These factors suggest that there is quite a distance from proclamations of taking back control and exiting with 'certainty, continuity and control' to a detailed view of what to do and how to reconcile the different objectives.

Before we look at the specifics of the UK government's Brexit objectives, it is useful to take a step back and clarify the nature of the UK's pre-Brexit EU relationship. The UK stands out in the sheer number and range of opt-outs and exemptions that it has obtained in its 45 years of EU membership: It is not part of the eurozone (is not part of the third stage of Monetary Union); is not part of the EU's banking union; is not part of the Schengen area; has opt-outs from justice and home affairs legislation (and opt-ins[5]); has some exemptions from the Charter of Fundamental Rights; and an opt-out from the EU's Working Time Directive (Adler-Nissen, 2014; Briggs, 2015). Opt-outs and exemptions are politically motivated. Those states seeking exemptions often do so to deflect domestic EU opposition/scepticism; the EU uses opt-outs and exemptions as a means of handling conflicts.

The number of opt-outs may give the impression that defining the scope and content of a state's relationship with the EU is purely a matter of political bargaining and political will. Some actors in the UK appear to view Brexit as an extension of this long tradition of the UK getting EU exemptions and opt-outs. To them, Brexit cannot be equated with secession (from a state) because they see the EU as something akin to a member state-run system of interstate bargaining. This is not the view we get from the EU institutions, which treat the process much more like a form of secession. When dealing with an outsider state, the EU is bound by its treaties that set clear limits to the kind of relationship the EU may enter into. This has been seen again and again, for example in the rejection by the Court of Justice of the first EEA Agreement, and on the conditions set by the court for the accession of the EU to the European Convention on Human Rights.[6]

For this book, we need to keep in mind the nature of the UK's EU relationship pre-Brexit, because in many instances the

UK has sought exemptions where Norway has sought inclusion. The UK's exemptions could make its EU relationship more similar to Norway's than to those of other EU members in selected issue areas. Or the opposite may be the case, namely that the UK's EU relationship is not only different from other EU members, but also from Norway's. We will clarify that as we go through the specifics of the Norway model in Chapters Three, Four and Five.

The UK government's objectives

Prime Minister Theresa May presented the government's position in her 17 January 2017 speech (May, 2017). She stated that her government would not seek to retain full access to the EU's internal market and customs union because that would entail reneging on control of immigration. The Government White Paper that spelled out the UK's objectives in detail stated that it:

> will prioritise securing the freest and most frictionless trade possible in goods and services between the UK and the EU. We will not be seeking membership of the Single Market, but will pursue instead a new strategic partnership with the EU, including an ambitious and comprehensive Free Trade Agreement and a new customs agreement. (UK Government, 2017b, 35)

May has consistently stated that this entails a bespoke deal or a deal that is different from such off-the-shelf arrangements as the EEA, the Comprehensive Economic and Trade Agreement (CETA) or even the Swiss model. An interesting point is that the focus on a bespoke deal is across the board – that is, well beyond access to the EU's internal market and customs union, including security, law enforcement and criminal justice. The UK government has produced a range of future partnership papers. In the one on security, law enforcement and criminal justice, it is stated that:

> [t]he UK and the EU should work together to design new, dynamic arrangements as part of the future partnership. Those arrangements should allow both parties to continue and strengthen their close collaboration on internal security – the areas of security, law enforcement and criminal justice – after the UK's withdrawal from the EU, drawing on long-standing shared traditions of respect for the rule of law and the protection of human rights. This would be a partnership that goes beyond the existing, often ad hoc arrangements for EU third-country relationships in this area, and draws on the legal models that the EU has used to structure cooperation with third countries in other fields, such as trade. It would involve identifying shared priorities for future cooperation and building new ways to facilitate cooperation on security, law enforcement and criminal justice. (UK Government, 2017c)

In a similar vein, in the areas of foreign policy and defence, the UK has pledged to continue to be a full partner. As May has noted: 'we want to play our part in making sure that Europe remains strong and prosperous and able to lead in the world, projecting its values and defending itself from security threats' (UK Government, 2017d). In the future partnership paper, these objectives were further spelled out, and it was underlined that the UK will together with the EU continue to promote a rules-based international order (UK Government, 2017e, 4).

The general impression is that the government has not settled the question of how to trade off sovereign control against assured EU access. The focus on bespoke agreements means on the one hand that much comes down to bargaining strength and acumen, and on the other that the process will need quite a bit of *time*. Guy Verhofstadt, the European Parliament's Brexit coordinator has criticised May's 'bespoke' concept. He has warned that '[t]he more complex and bespoke the future agreement is, the longer it will take to agree and the greater the risk of further uncertainty' (Murphy, 2017).

There have been shifts in the UK government's position. We get some sense of the distance that the government has travelled since May's Lancaster House speech in January 2017 by drawing on the comprehensive overview of the process of Brexit that Alan Renwick offered not long after the PM's speech and comparing that to the present. He then presented the following options:

- First, a comprehensive deal covering both the terms of Brexit and the detailed terms of the UK's future relationship with the EU;
- second, a deal on withdrawal terms that is combined with transitional arrangements that tide matters over while the future relationship is determined;
- third, a deal on withdrawal terms only, with negotiations on the future relationship conducted after withdrawal, but without any transitional arrangements in place during that period;
- fourth, no deal, with Brexit taking place after two years (or longer if an extension has been agreed) via the automatic provision set out in Article 50 (3);
- finally, a decision for the UK to stay within the EU after all. (Renwick, 2017, 9)

Out of these, the May government in January 2017 stated that it preferred the first: a hard Brexit that resolved all major issues simultaneously. The EU preferred the second option, which entails a two-stage process: settle the terms of exit first and thereafter settle the terms of the new form of association between the UK and the EU. That option is sensitive to the time requirements involved and brings up the question of whether the UK would be able to settle its future relationship with the

EU within the two-year negotiation period. The third option is the quintessential 'hard Brexit', which would subject the UK to WTO rules (dependent on negotiations with the WTO), and the possible reintroduction of tariffs. The fourth option is disorderly Brexit. The fifth option is that Brexit may not in the end come about.

Objectives and the process of negotiations

When the negotiations started, it became apparent that the EU's two-stage approach had won out. The EU insisted on the need to settle the terms of exit (notably pertaining to citizens' rights, financial obligations and the Northern Ireland border question) *before* negotiating the terms of the UK's future EU relationship. The EU has since then monitored on an ongoing basis whether there is enough progress in the negotiations to start the second stage of negotiations, thus putting pressure on the UK government to come to terms with the EU's financial and other demands. There is little doubt that this structuring of the negotiations has given the EU the upper hand (Eeckhout and Patel, 2017), as is also clearly reflected in the Withdrawal Agreement.

In late April 2017, Prime Minister May made a surprise announcement for a June election. The Conservatives had a strong lead in the polls and wanted to capitalise on this lead so that May would have a stronger parliamentary support base in the upcoming Brexit negotiations. May underlined the need for strong and stable leadership. Echoing this, Greg Knight, Conservative candidate for East Yorkshire, summed up the choice in the following manner: 'We want a strong and stable government, not a coalition of chaos, led by Jeremy Corbyn' (Rodgers, 2017). The election result went in the opposite direction: the Conservatives lost their majority in the House of Commons.[7] In order to remain in power they formed a deal with the Democratic Unionist Party of Northern Ireland, which agreed to support the Conservatives in parliament (although this agreement still had to be agreed by the House of Commons). Insofar as the 8 June election can be seen as the public's verdict on Brexit, the result meant greater support for a 'soft' Brexit, and for some form of transition agreement with the EU.

There is little doubt that the UK government's recognition of the need for a transition deal has served to bring the EEA Agreement back on the agenda as one of the possible (temporary) resting places on the UK's Brexit journey. In connection with that, there is a debate on whether the UK can remain in the EEA when Brexit has formally taken place (after the Article 50 TEU deadline of 29 March 2019 has expired, which entails that the UK leaves the EU). We will comment on this debate in Chapter Six.

A transition arrangement can be structured along a number of different lines, as was clearly outlined in a recent paper by Eeckhout and Patel (2017). They present the following five options:

1. extension of the EU *acquis communautaire*, without membership;
2. an extension of the Article 50 withdrawal negotiations;
3. remaining in the internal market via the EEA Agreement;
4. remaining in the internal market by negotiating a new agreement modelled on the EEA Agreement;
5. entering into a customs agreement with the EU customs union.

Their assessment is that the first option is the most desirable because it entails the least amount of disruption, but this option privileges access over sovereign *political* control. It resembles the Norway model in the sense that this is what the Norway model entails in practice (NOU 2012:2; Eriksen and Fossum, 2015). The second option is also simple in practice because it is about extending the present situation, but it is likely to be politically difficult in the EU and in particular in the UK. It starts to be all about appearances, but ironically, in contrast to the first option, the UK will retain an element of control. The third option entails that the UK will have to apply for membership in EFTA, as a precondition for joining EEA (all EEA countries that are not EU members are members of EFTA). For the UK, one problematic aspect would be that the EEA countries are not part of the EU's customs union, which means that the UK would need to find ways to work out the problems for its manufacturing sector as it relies on import of foreign components. An advantage of this arrangement for the UK would be that EEA countries are free to sign trade agreements with other states. The EEA removes some issue areas from EU purview; hence it represents a somewhat different balance of sovereign control and access than does full membership, but as we will show in the chapters on the Norway model, even in those issue areas that are formally removed from the EEA Agreement, the EU wields significant control of activities. The fourth option may be so tailored as to be more suitable to the UK than the present EEA Agreement, but it brings up a number of questions of design and the degree to which there is political willingness on the two sides to develop suitable institutional arrangements. The fifth and final option tilts the balance between control and access somewhat, but if we use the EU-Turkey customs union as the template – as Eeckhout and Patel (2017) do – then the UK would lose out on both control and access under this option (although Hammond has suggested that this might be a possibility[8]).

A factor that points towards a solution along the same lines as the Norway model (plus customs union) is the declaration on Ireland and Northern Ireland in the Joint Report from the negotiators of the European Union and the United Kingdom government on progress during phase 1 of negotiations under Article 50 TEU on the United Kingdom's withdrawal from the European Union (European Commission, 2017a). According to Articles 49 and 50 the United Kingdom 'will maintain full alignment with those rules of the Internal Market and the Customs Union which, now or in the future, support North–South cooperation', and 'will continue to ensure the same unfettered access for Northern Ireland's businesses to the whole of the United Kingdom internal market' (European Commission, 2017a). In practice, this amounts to some sort of solution that entails maintaining the regulatory conditions necessary for participation in the single market, both for Northern Ireland and for the rest of the UK. Irish Prime Minister Leo Varadkar understood this as a cast-iron commitment to the effect that there would be no hard border – in other words that 'maintain' refers to keeping things as they are now. The agreement accentuates the need for the UK in its future arrangements with the EU to find solutions to the question of how to trade off sovereign control with assured EU access.

The European Council 15 December 2017 Conclusions states that the European Council 'agrees to negotiate a transition period covering the whole of the EU *acquis*, while the United Kingdom, as a third country, will no longer participate in or nominate or elect, members of the EU institutions, nor participate in the decision-making of the Union bodies, offices, and agencies' (European Council, 2017, 1). That is akin to the first option as previously discussed.

Positions

The UK government started the process towards Brexit by stating that Brexit means Brexit. The government asserted that there would be no cliff-edge. But May also stated that no deal is better than a bad deal. That has to be seen in light of the fact that the government considered all off-the-shelf arrangements as bad deals. We have sought to detail how the government's position has shifted towards a softer Brexit in light of the effects of the June election and other events that weakened the May government's control and steering of the process. The government sought to keep tight control of the process, but has had to yield to various pressures for access and influence as the process proceeded.

There are speculations as to how long the May government will last. If there is a change in government, as the analysis of the different positions will show, the process and the outcome will definitely be affected. In Figure 1.1 we illustrate that there are many different alternatives. In addition, the parties are internally divided; thus it is difficult to associate a given Brexit outcome with any one of the four main options outlined (hence we have left the entries blank). Even within each option, it matters what type of support the government has. For instance, whether a Conservative majority government is based on its own support or relies on a coalition.

Figure 1.1: Possible government constellations

	Majority government (On its own/coalition)	Minority government
Labour		
Conservative		

We present these options in order to underline that the process can be tracked along quite different directions should there be a change in government. The different possible positions will become more apparent when we consider what objectives the main actors have. We focus here on those actors that we assume are most capable of influencing – blocking or altering – the government's preferred course of action.

Parliament and the political parties

With regard to parliament's influence on the Brexit option that the UK should end up with and how that should be obtained, two aspects require particular attention. The first is that the core objective of Brexit was to 'take back control', which effectively meant to transfer power back from EU institutions to popularly elected and accountable British ones. As Prime Minister May noted in her Florence speech in September 2017: 'the British electorate made a choice. They chose the power of domestic democratic control over pooling that control, strengthening the role of the UK Parliament and the devolved Scottish Parliament, Welsh and Northern Ireland Assemblies in deciding our laws' (UK Government, 2017f). Parliament soon discovered that there was a significant gap between statements and facts, as shown above: May sought to retain central governmental control of the Brexit process and did not envisage a very prominent role for any of the popularly elected representative bodies that she listed in her speech. The two houses of the UK Parliament (and the national devolved administrations' assemblies, as we will show below) have actively sought to assert themselves as active players in the process with the will and the ability to shape and direct this, including obtaining a meaningful say on the final Brexit agreement.

The UK Parliament (not the national devolved administrations' assemblies) was aided in this undertaking by the Supreme Court's 24 January 2017 Miller decision (UK Supreme Court, 2017a). The decision pertained to whether the UK government could use its prerogative powers to withdraw from the EU, or whether that required prior authorisation by parliament (through an act of parliament). In an accompanying statement, the Supreme Court states (by a majority of eight against three) 'that an Act of Parliament is required to authorise ministers to give Notice of the decision of the UK to withdraw from the European Union' (UK Supreme Court, 2017b). Parliament has since then actively sought to shape the European Union (Withdrawal) Bill and is at the time of writing engaged in a struggle to obtain a significant role in the process of ratifying whatever agreement the UK negotiates with the EU.

The second aspect and an important additional reason for parliamentary activism is the fact of political disagreement between government and (large portions of) parliament on the substantive nature of the Brexit decision – in other words, the nature of the UK's terms of exit and its future settlement with the EU. There was after all a significant majority of Remainers in the UK Parliament prior to the June 2017 election.[9] The election campaign was not fought over Brexit; both major parties had made clear that they would respect the result of the popular referendum. The election outcome strengthened the number of voters behind both major parties (though for the Conservatives that did not translate into number of seats) but did in overall terms mark a shift towards a softer form of Brexit (Ford, 2017). For Labour, which did not initially articulate a very clear position on what option to go for, the shift appeared over the summer. The most explicit statements were made by Labour's Keir Starmer, shadow Brexit minister, who noted that Labour sought 'a new, progressive partnership with the EU' that mirrored single market benefits (Walker et al, 2017). Starmer said remaining in a customs union in the EU was 'a possible end destination for Labour' (Walker et al, 2017). He also said that 'we are flexible as to whether the benefits of the single market are best retained by negotiating a new single market relationship or by working up from a bespoke trade deal... No rash, ideological red lines preventing a sensible deal' (Walker et al, 2017). Some Labour MPs have since been more explicit with regard to the EEA. Stephen Kinnock noted in the 6 November 2017 House of Commons debate on the EEA:

> Given that an off-the-shelf transition deal is inevitable, it is clear to me that EEA-EFTA is the only option. The EEA and EFTA are well-established and well-understood arrangements that offer the clarity, stability and predictability that the British economy so desperately needs in these turbulent times. Transferring from the EU to

the EEA and EFTA would allow us to balance sovereignty and market access. Crucially, such a transition deal would buy us time [to] negotiate the final comprehensive trade and strategic partnership deal that will shape the terms of the UK's relationship with the EU for decades to come, while also allowing us to enter into independent trade negotiations with third countries because we would be outside the customs union. (UK Parliament, 2017a)

This short overview shows that parliament is playing a central role in shaping the process and has assumed a more significant role as the process has proceeded, even if the executive imprint is bound to be very strong. The extent to which parliament will serve as a veto actor is a matter currently under discussion in terms of how much say it will have on the final agreement with the EU (Asthana, 2017). The UK Parliament's efforts to influence the process and outcome find strong resonance with the national devolved administrations' assemblies and their governments.

The devolved nations

The UK is often referred to as a pluri-national state (Keating, 2001), with important powers and competencies devolved to the regional level, and where national devolved administration assemblies in Scotland, Wales and Northern Ireland have emerged as important democratic actors, with claims to power and legitimacy. The UK is an asymmetrical state in the sense that there is no assembly or parliament for England; the UK Parliament represents all of the UK as well as England. What is important to keep in mind in connection with Brexit is that the devolved settlements are based primarily on the delivery of EU legislation within the UK. The nations have no role in EU negotiations but are responsible for delivery. That is why Brexit is so fundamental to them. Also they rest on the principle of subsidiarity. If the UK leaves the EU, the parliament and assemblies can only be guaranteed for five years at a time – the length of a parliamentary term – as no parliament can fetter the next one in the UK constitution. The nations have developed their own relationships with the EU. These nations depend on EU exports more than does England, and they also benefit more from EU spending than does England. The three nations all seek to remain within the EU's single market and are more supportive of immigration than the UK government. There is therefore a lot at stake for the nations in terms of the process and substance of Brexit. When it comes to influence, they, like all regions/regional nations across Europe, lack direct access to the EU's main decision-making bodies (European Council and Council formations); their main channel of influence therefore remains the national level. In connection with Brexit, they joined the Miller suit and argued that Brexit would require consent of the devolved legislatures. The Supreme Court rejected that claim, however. Since then it has become clear that legislative consent motions will be required in Scotland and Wales before Brexit can proceed.

Domestically, the main instruments for regional influence are the Joint Ministerial Committees (JMCs), which have no statutory basis, but are based on a memorandum of understanding and supplementary agreements. In connection with Brexit, a new structure, the JMC for European Negotiations, has been formed. There are bilateral contacts, at the level of government officials and at ministerial level. Different parties in the different nations render this ineffective. There is quite a lot of activity in many of the issue areas that have been devolved: agriculture, the environment, fisheries and cohesion policy. Nevertheless:

the intra-UK structures for the devolved administrations to influence UK foreign policy in this area have proven rather weak and ineffective. There is little evidence to indicate that the devolved administrations have succeeded in getting their policy priorities accepted, nor has there been a positive response from the UK Government to their requests to be included at the table once negotiations begin. (Hunt and Minto, 2017, 654)

However, there is evidence that officials are working together effectively through task groups established by the British–Irish Council (Morphet and Clifford 2018).

With regard to Scotland, it voted overwhelmingly in favour of remain and is 'determined to maintain Scotland's position in the European Single Market' (Government of Scotland, 2016, vi). Scotland prefers a soft Brexit and an arrangement as close to the Norway model as possible; it wants to be within the EEA and the customs union. Since the EEA countries are not part of the customs union, we could label this mode of affiliation EEA+. Scotland has also brought up the prospect of a differentiated arrangement by noting that the UK government itself seeks different arrangements for the various sectors and that other actors (mayor of London) seek special arrangements with the EU on immigration. Scotland does not prioritise access to the single market over free trade and free movement within the UK. Nevertheless, Scotland may opt for a new independence referendum if the UK 'takes Scotland out of the EU against its will' (Government of Scotland, 2016, vi).

With regard to Wales, it voted in favour of leave, but in its January 2017 White Paper the Welsh government expressed a preference for continued UK participation in the single market (Hunt and Minto, 2017, 652), for instance through membership in EFTA. Wales is in many ways squeezed between Brussels and London. It is a net beneficiary of the EU's Common Agricultural Policy (CAP) and structural funds, but underlines the importance of a 'one-UK Brexit' and stresses the need for loyal cooperation with Westminster.

With regard to Northern Ireland, a majority of the voters were in favour of Remain. It is noteworthy that '[t]he vote was mainly, if not entirely, along nationalist/unionist lines, confirming an old division: unionists were staking a "British" identity by voting Leave, and nationalists an Irish one by voting Remain' (Gormley-Heenan and Aughey, 2017, 497). If the UK ends up with a bespoke agreement that entails leaving the single market and customs union, a new border will emerge on the island of Ireland. The ensuing fear is that Brexit may undermine the foundations of the Good Friday Agreement (sometimes known as the Belfast Agreement) reached on 10 April 1998 by the United Kingdom government, the Irish government and the other participants in the multi-party negotiations (the '1998 Agreement') by bringing forth a binary choice between an open Irish border and an open UK border. Finding a solution to the Northern Ireland border problem was thus one of the three main items that were addressed in the exit negotiations. The problem is compounded by the fact that 'North-South cooperation relies to a significant extent on a common European Union legal and policy framework. Therefore, the United Kingdom's departure from the European Union gives rise to substantial challenges to the maintenance and development of North-South cooperation' (European Commission, 2017a, 7-8). As mentioned, the 8 December Joint Report from the negotiators of the European Union and the United Kingdom government ensures that the UK will maintain full alignment with those rules of the internal market and the customs union which, now or in the future, support North-South cooperation, and will continue to ensure the same unfettered access for Northern Ireland's businesses to the whole of the United Kingdom internal market. The Prime Minister has also confirmed that there will be no East-West border in the Irish Sea, suggesting the status quo, with obvious parallels to the Norway option.

Business actors

The Confederation of British Industry (CBI), the City and other large UK firms wanted the UK to remain in the EU. Pre-Brexit we may speak of a kind of synthesis of business and state power within the UK directed against EU social and employment policy. In effect, '[t]wo distinct objectives have ... underpinned the strategic orientation of British business in relation to European integration since the 1990s: to *defend* the United Kingdom's liberal labour market regime from supranational encroachment and to *extend* a liberalising bias outwards into the wider framework of European capitalism' (Lavery, 2017, 699). For these important business actors, Brexit represents a double bind. On the one hand they risk losing market access as a consequence of a hard Brexit or if no agreement is found. On the other hand, even a soft Brexit or a situation that moves the UK to a rule taker will mean that they lose control of their important historical role in influencing the terms of economic interaction in Europe. This is clearly far more than market access. The tables then turn from actively seeking to promote the UK's model across Europe by setting the terms of economic interaction to actively seeking to defend the UK's liberal model against supranational EU incursions, whether the UK is formally incorporated in the EU or not. We would generally consider business a veto actor because it can use investment and (re) location strategically to promote its interests. However, it is not clear how attentive Brexiteers are to their concerns, as some Brexiteers seem quite ideologically driven.

There are signs that business activism is on the rise. Carolyn Fairbairn of the CBI recently noted that: '[w]e remain extremely worried and the clock carries on ticking down'. As a result, she said, more 'and more firms are triggering their contingency plans to move jobs or change investment plans' (UK Parliament, 2017a). There have been numerous requests for sectorial deals in areas such as agriculture, automotive hospitality and health.

Trade unions

The UK Trade Union Congress (TUC) is also committed to a policy of sustaining UK membership of the EU's single market and customs union, as this mode of affiliation is considered the best way of protecting British workers after Brexit. The TUC has been among the actors putting pressure on Corbyn's Labour to come clear on support for the single market (Stewart, 2017).

This brief overview of the government's objectives and a select number of other actors shows that the initial populist-inspired focus on a hard Brexit faces strong opposition from many quarters. The actors have different interests, a case in point being the different positions that business and labour unions hold on workers' rights, but they all seem to converge on the need for some form of soft Brexit that ensures continued access to the EU's internal market, whether through an off-the-shelf or a bespoke agreement.

The UK's EU encoding

The UK is deeply EU encoded after 45 years of EU membership, reinforced by the fact that the UK's efficient administration makes it a very effective implementer of EU legislation. In the context of Brexit, the EU imprint on the UK is clearly visible in the sheer scale and scope of the European Union Withdrawal Bill: if the UK is to 'take back control' it has to relate to the impressive body of EU rules, norms and regulations that the UK has incorporated – over 12,000 (UK Parliament, 2017b). The purpose of this bill is to prevent a cliff-edge, but as numerous commentators have already noted, the bill raises a number of thorny questions, not the least pertaining to parliamentary sovereignty given its extensive reliance on so-called Henry VIII powers, whereby secondary legislation is used to amend primary legislation (Elliott, 2017[10]). The inclusion of broad and widely scoped delegated powers to ministers as a means of ensuring flexibility will represent a significant transfer of power to the executive. The Brexit objective of taking back control would then benefit the UK executive at the expense of the parliament. The bill will not transfer powers to the devolved nations but instead divert them to the central government which would then decide how to deal with them. That is also why nations such as Scotland and Wales have asserted that they will not recommend that legislative consent be given to the bill. Finally, since the bill provides the government with extensive powers to amend law (including Henry VIII powers), the bill can be used to effect significant policy changes, thus raising questions as to the very notions of certainty, continuity and control that it is supposed to ensure.

The European Union

Brexit appears at a point in time when the EU is fraught with challenges, pertaining to the lingering effects of the financial crisis, the rise of authoritarianism within and outside its borders, regime collapses and possibilities of sudden influxes of large numbers of immigrants and asylum seekers, and the rise of Eurosceptic right-wing populist parties and movements. The sum total of these crises and challenges suggested that the EU would operate as a weak and quite fragmented opponent to the British government. Thus far, it is the opposite – on the one hand the EU has displayed unity, and on the other it has formulated a set of quite detailed guidelines for the negotiations, as well as an institutional division of powers in the management of the negotiations. The core body in charge is the European Council, which issues the negotiation guidelines, monitors progress and determines the structure of the negotiations, including when the second stage will start. The Commission is in charge of the ongoing negotiations, and reports to the European Council. Non-members, such as the EEA states, are not part of the negotiations. As noted above, the EU insisted on the need to conduct the negotiations in two stages: negotiate the divorce settlement first, and then the new terms of association; and monitor progress in stage one before the second stage is activated.

The EU talks about and treats Brexit as a divorce in terms more similar to the breakup of a state than as the voluntary withdrawal of a member from a loosely knit confederation of states. In that sense, there is a difference in perspective across the Channel: it is quite common in the UK to depict the EU as a loose confederation of states (even if some Brexiteers conjure up the image of the EU as a federal superstate), whereas the EU operates more as a federation of states. This is amplified by the notion that the EU embodies a certain socioeconomic model or vision which seeks to balance market with environmental and social concerns. The EU's chief negotiator Michel Barnier recently said:

> The UK has chosen to leave the EU. Does it want to stay close to the European model or does it want to gradually move away from it? The UK's reply to this question will be important and even decisive because it will shape the discussion on our future partnership and shape also the conditions for ratification of that partnership in many national parliaments and obviously in the European parliament. I do not say this to create problems but to avoid problems. (European Commission, 2017b)

Concluding reflections

This chapter has shown that the UK government has struggled to find a viable approach to handling the Brexit decision. The referendum did not and could not give a clear steer to the subsequent direction. The government sought to exert control but has had to give way to numerous pressures from a range of quarters. It is also readily apparent that the government has yielded numerous concessions to the EU on the way. If we look at the text of the Withdrawal Agreement, we see that the UK government has conceded on all three points of the exit negotiations: EU budget contributions, the rights of EU citizens, and the Northern Ireland border situation. The UK government pinned its hopes on a bargaining strategy aimed at creating bespoke agreements across a range of issue areas and institutional realms. That has proven to be a very difficult strategy for reasons of time and since it was apparent for all to see that it would forfeit access and any element of predictability. If we put it bluntly the UK government sought a bargaining approach, whereas the EU was far more bent on developing and following rules and procedures. Thus far, there is no question which approach has won out.

How these developments translate to the UK's relationship to the Norway model remains shrouded in uncertainty but some patterns are emerging. It is quite clear that the UK government's outright dismissal of the Norway model is more at a rhetorical than a practical level, especially with regard to a transitional arrangement where the UK most likely will remain subject to EU rules and norms but without any influence. Politically speaking this will resemble Norway's position; legally speaking the UK will most likely continue to be subject to EU institutions, including the CJEU. The 8 December Joint Report from the negotiators of the European Union and the United Kingdom government on citizens' rights and the arrangements for their consistent interpretation points in this direction.

There is nothing to suggest that there will be a direct and outright embrace of the Norway model. If that is so, the subsequent negotiations will show how close to or far away from that model it will end up. There is recognition in many quarters that the UK needs to be included in the EU's customs union; hence suggesting a role for the Norwegian option plus. The agreement on Ireland already goes far in prompting this. At the same time, the UK has a number of EU exceptions that Norway does not have; thus in issue areas outside of the internal market it is likely to be a matter of the Norwegian option minus. We cannot rule out that the transition may involve a pick-and-mix approach to elements of the Norway model. Given the UK government's initial intransigence, we are likely to see a disguised adoption of these elements of the Norway model.

2

Forms of affiliation with non-members

This chapter provides a brief overview of the EU's range of affiliations with non-members. The purpose of the chapter is threefold. First, the aim is to show that while the EU has elements of stateness – as Genschel and Jachtenfuchs (2014) note, it has moved into core state powers and the member states lend it their stateness – it has developed a distinct approach to borders and bordering that greatly conditions its relations to members and non-members, regardless of the type of affiliation involved. That shows an EU readiness to adapt its relations to its surroundings, and is clearly of relevance for the UK government's focus on bespoke agreements. Whereas the EU is adaptive to its surroundings, it is not without principles and even strict legal rules. There are guidelines, frameworks and clear legal limits that shape how the EU fashions its external relations, which reflect back on the EU's structure and self-conception as a legal and political system, including its approach to borders and bordering. We need to pay attention to the EU's treaties as well as its principles and guidelines in order to get a handle on the wiggle-room that is available for non-members.

The second purpose of the chapter is to provide a brief overview of the sheer range of off-the-shelf modes of affiliation already out there. It is beyond the scope of this book to provide a set of compelling explanations for the nature and range of this broad spectrum of EU affiliations. What is readily apparent is that there are so many and such diverse states bordering the EU that it is difficult to imagine this diversity will not also shape the EU's external relations.

The third and final purpose of the chapter is to zoom in on and provide a brief overview of the Swiss model. This chapter thus helps to conceptualise the discussion of the Norway model as one among a broad range of modes of affiliation.

The EU and the question of borders and bordering

The EU's openness to its surroundings is apparent in the fact that membership is possible for all European states (even if it is readily apparent that some long-term applicants such as Turkey are unlikely ever to become members), though EU membership is conditional on compliance with a range of criteria, namely the so-called Copenhagen criteria.[11] The question of conditionality and compliance with EU rules and norms does not stop at the EU's borders however; states can operate in accordance with EU rules and norms without being EU members. The implication is that in the EU, on the one hand, we need to think of borders in terms of formal membership: which states are members and which are not. On the other hand, we need to think of borders with reference to functions, because EU rules and norms regulate functions within and outside the EU's member states. In the EU, the territorial reach of functions varies, and the same applies to the functional breadth of a given territorial configuration. Consider the differences in territorial reach of, respectively, the euro area, the EEA, the EU's customs union and Schengen.

In an EU context, therefore, the issue of borders and bordering differs from how we are conditioned to think of borders as per the classical conception of state sovereignty (not the reality of existing states), as a manifestation of territorial and functional *contiguity* or correspondence. The EU differs but subject to important conditions, or what we may refer to as conditionality. Non-members can always approximate to EU policies and laws unilaterally. But if non-members want any commitment from the EU – either to give them some say in the making of EU policies or laws or to work together to ensure convergence – the EU has to decide under what *conditions* it is able to commit itself to non-members in those ways. Since the EU has such an extensive system of arrangements with non-members, it is useful to consider conditionality as an intrinsic element of how to think about borders and bordering. In the extension of that, the following three features depict how the EU constitutes its relations to its members and *affiliated* non-members. First, formal EU membership provides the member states with *direct access* to all the relevant decision opportunities within the complex EU structure (primarily a seat in the European Council; direct representation in the Council of Ministers formations; direct representation in the European Parliament; and direct presence in the system of comitology). That right is reserved for EU members. Second, non-members *may incorporate* EU norms and rules, but subject to conditionality and compliance requirements. This may include a limited form of non-decision-relevant access, as in the EEA (Fossum, 2015). Third, what appears to be the underlying principle, the closer (in breadth and depth terms) the affiliation, *the stricter the requirements*. This last point serves to underline that the EU's relationship to affiliated non-members is all but voluntaristic. States that seek an affiliation with the EU cannot unilaterally determine their relationship to the EU; the EU sets down quite explicit conditions for the relevant types of access (to what functions and territories), and insists on mechanisms to ensure that states operate in accordance with what they have committed themselves to do in relation to the EU. Another way of putting this is to say that the EU is concerned with preventing its external relations – forms of affiliation with non-members – destabilising internal coherence, weakening policy consistency or undermining the autonomy and integrity of EU law.

The non-members for their part face the need for balancing ensured access to the EU's internal market and the other policies that the EU regulates, on the one hand, and retaining domestic control of what is taking place within their territories (and beyond) on the other. The basic considerations that animate actors differ considerably. The structure of the association suggests that the EU for its part will seek to limit the non-members' room for manoeuvre, harmonise and unify the various relations it has with the external world, and ensure that those affiliated fulfil their obligations, whereas the affiliated states will seek to maximise their room for manoeuvre, obtain special treatment, and avoid as much external binding and control as possible.

To sum up thus far, the EU has shifted the relationship between state sovereign control, national democracy and assured market (and other forms of) access. There is an important shift in the equation for affiliated states but it is not the same as for members and it varies across types of affiliated non-members.

In the following, we will briefly introduce each of the forms of EU affiliation with non-members and thereafter clarify the core issues and concerns of relevance for the discussion of Brexit and the EU's non-members. When discussing these affiliation arrangements in relation to Brexit, we need to keep in mind an important distinction between those non-member states that *qualify* for EU membership, but have declined membership (or have failed to apply for it), and those states that *do not qualify* for EU membership. The latter category will include states that may become EU members in the future, as well as states that may never be. The UK, being 'EU encoded' through 45 years of

EU membership, will definitely belong to the former category, not the least given that the UK will pass its European Union Withdrawal Bill, which, apart from repealing the 1972 European Communities Act, also incorporates almost all present EU legislation into UK law. The other reason is that the EU is more willing to give access to states that qualify for EU membership.

Different forms of EU affiliation

With regard to states that do not qualify for EU membership, there are four main forms of affiliation: the European Neighbourhood Policy (ENP), Turkey's customs union, the position of the small European countries, and sectoral multilateralism such as the Energy Community Treaty (Gstöhl, 2015). The two latter are clearly not relevant in a Brexit context. Nor is the EU's Neighbourhood Policy, which was initiated in 2004. It provides Eastern and Southern Mediterranean countries with enhanced preferential trade relations, they receive financial and technical assistance and 'the prospect of a stake in the EU Internal Market based on legislative and regulatory approximation, the participation in a number of EU programmes and improved interconnection and physical links with the EU' (Gstöhl, 2015, 18). Even if the Mediterranean countries thus become subject to a comprehensive market access conditionality there is no presumption that this will lead to future EU membership (in contrast to what may be the case for Eastern European countries). The Turkey model has been discussed in the UK setting in connection with Brexit (UK Government, 2016). Turkey is both an EU candidate country (since 1999), and has participated in a customs union with the EU since 1995. This model does not appear to be suitable for the UK because it gives Turkey only selective access to the EU's internal market, which does not include services, provides no say on the decisions affecting it, and lacks reciprocity with regard to EU trade agreements with third countries. As the UK government position paper notes:

> we would lose our decision-making power over the UK's external tariffs, because we would be part of the Customs Union. Instead, we would be forced to open our borders to countries with which the EU had agreed trade deals, without necessarily being able to secure reciprocal access. Such a situation would put the UK economy at a substantial disadvantage. (UK Government, 2016, 30)

There is an important difference between being a member of *the* EU's customs union, on the one hand, and on the other hand being a member of *a* customs union. After Brexit, the UK cannot be a member of the EU's customs union.

None of the options available for affiliated states that fail to qualify as EU members appears relevant for the UK. These states are also less closely affiliated with the UK than are those that qualify for EU membership.

The Swiss model

Turning now to affiliation agreements that the EU has with countries that would qualify for membership, Switzerland turned down EEA membership in 1992 after a negative referendum. It has instead established a set of bilateral agreements with the EU. Switzerland's EU relationship is centred on two sets of bilateral agreements, which are labelled Bilateral I (entered into force in 2002) and Bilateral II (signed in 2004 and gradually implemented since). In addition, Switzerland and the EU have a large number of other agreements, in total about 120 (see Appendix I). These agreements do not take over the *acquis* of the single market *en bloc*, but are limited to positively listed areas and freedoms. The freedom to be taken over most comprehensively is the free movement of persons. In addition, the agreements include notably land and air transport, public procurement, agricultural products, environment, science and technology and double taxation. Switzerland also participates in the Schengen and Dublin agreements, and there are various other agreements on administrative assistance and cooperation. Apart from the Schengen and Dublin agreements and the one on air transport, the agreements do not entail a takeover of the EU *acquis*.

The agreement on the free movement of persons is part of the Bilateral I package. It gives nationals of the member states of the European Community and Switzerland a right of entry, residence, access to work as employed persons, establishment on a self-employed basis and the right to stay in the territory of the contracting parties. Entailed in the right to free movement is the right to establishment. Since the right to establishment is part of the right to free movement of persons, it does not extend to legal bodies (se Case C-351/08: Official Journal of the European Communities, 2009). The right to free movement of persons also entails the right to provide services, but only for 'a brief duration', limited to 90 days of actual work in a calendar year (Official Journal of the European Communities, 2002a, Article 5).

The agreements are formally speaking *static sectoral agreements*, which add up to 20 main and over 100 secondary agreements, without an overarching structure binding them together. One of the main reasons for the Swiss rejection of the EEA Agreement in the referendum of 1992 was the dynamic character of the EEA. Switzerland's EU relationship is nevertheless quite dynamic, not the least since Swiss authorities have since the late 1980s operated with the doctrine of '*autonomer Nachvollzug*', which refers to autonomous adaptation and represents a policy of voluntary alignment with the EU. This doctrine 'stipulates that each new piece of legislation is evaluated with respect to its compatibility with EU norms' (Lavenex, 2009, 552). In a similar manner, Alfred Tovias (2006) noted ten years ago that 'Switzerland has had an EC reflex for more than a decade now and tries to shadow EU moves autonomously. Because this process is invisible and silent, it is frequently but wrongly ignored' (Tovias, 2006, 215). Leaked documents from the ongoing EU–Swiss negotiations reveal that the EU seeks to impose much stricter legal obligations on Switzerland (Piris, 2017).

The Swiss agreements contain provisions to achieve homogeneity in the application of the rules in Switzerland and the EU. The agreements in Bilateral Package 1 are tied together with a so-called *Guillotine Clause* that makes the agreements dependent on each other. For instance, Article 36 (4) of the agreement on air traffic states that 'the seven agreements referred to in paragraph 1 shall cease to be applicable six months after receipt of the notification of non-renewal'. Also, the Schengen and the Dublin agreements are tied together in this manner. The agreements further have provisions on the inclusion of new legislation into the agreements, and the right of the other party to adopt safeguard measures if a party refuses to agree to the inclusion of new legislation. Although formally reciprocal, the provisions are mechanisms to include new or amended EU legislation in the agreements.

When it comes to judicial homogeneity, the agreements on free movement of persons and on air traffic contain a clause on the relevance of the case law of the CJEU. For instance, Article 16 (2) of the agreement between the European Community and the Swiss Confederation on the free movement of persons, states:

> Insofar as the application of this Agreement involves concepts of Community law, account shall be taken of the relevant case-law of the Court of Justice of the European Communities prior to the date of its signature. Case-law after this date shall be brought to Switzerland's attention. To ensure that the Agreement works properly, the Joint Committee shall, at the request of either Contracting

Party, determine the implications of such case-law. (Official
Journal of the European Communities, 2002a)[12]

Even agreements that do not contain such a clause must as far
as possible be interpreted in accordance with the case law of the
CJEU (Kaddous, 2014, 962). Article 16 (2) of the agreement
on the free movement of persons is similar to the provisions
of the EEA Agreement Article 6 and Surveillance and Court
Agreement (SCA) Article 3. For decisions by the Court of
Justice given prior to the date of signature, the arrangements are
identical. When it comes to later rulings, there are differences.
The SCA Article 3.2 states that the EFTA Court and EFTA
Surveillance Authority (ESA) 'shall pay due account' (Official
Journal of the European Communities, 1994a) whereas the
Swiss agreements go no further than stating that these rulings
'shall be communicated to Switzerland' (Official Journal of the
European Communities, 2002a, 2002b). If one of the parties
requests it, 'the implications of such latter rulings and decisions
shall be determined by the Joint Committee in view of ensuring
the proper functioning of this Agreement' (Official Journal of
the European Communities 2002b). This means that the Swiss
agreements leave the resolution of differences in interpretation
to a political solution, whereas the EEA Agreement provides
arrangements to solve the issue by judicial means.

Seeing that the interpretation of the agreement takes place in
different courts that are independent of each other, differences
may arise also within the EEA. Therefore, EEA Article 105
states that the EEA Committee 'shall keep under constant
review the development of the case law of the Court of Justice
of the European Communities and the EFTA Court', and take
measures 'to preserve the homogeneous interpretation of the
Agreement' (Official Journal of the European Communities,
1994b). Article 106 states that:

In order to ensure as uniform an interpretation as possible of this Agreement, in full deference to the independence of courts, a system of exchange of information concerning judgments by the EFTA Court, the Court of Justice of the European Communities and the Court of First Instance of the European Communities and the Courts of last instance of the EFTA States shall be set up by the EEA Joint Committee. (Official Journal of the European Communities, 1994b)

In the event of differences or disputes over the interpretation of the agreement, EEA Article 111 empowers the EEA Joint Committee to settle the dispute according to principles laid down in that article. Thus, we see that, in the final instance, also in the EEA the settlement of disputes over interpretation is political and not judicial.

The principles according to which the agreements are interpreted also differ. In a consistent line of cases, the CJEU has stated that the interpretation given to the provisions of European Union law concerning the internal market cannot automatically be applied by analogy to the interpretation of the Swiss agreements. The first case, Case C-351/08 *Grimme*, raised the question of whether the agreement on free movement of persons, which provided for the right of establishment for people could be extended to legal bodies (Official Journal of the European Union, 2009). The court rejected this. For its interpretation of the agreement, the court took as its starting point that:

The Swiss Confederation, by its refusal, did not subscribe to the project of an economically integrated entity with a single market, based on common rules between its members, but chose the route of bilateral arrangements between the Community and its Member States in specific areas. Therefore, the Swiss Confederation did not join the internal market of the Community the aim of which is the removal of all obstacles to create an area of total freedom of movement analogous to that provided by a national market, which includes inter alia the freedom to provide services and the freedom of establishment (paragraph 27). (Official Journal of the European Union, 2013, 78-9)

This means that interpretation of the provisions of European Union law, including treaty provisions, concerning the internal market cannot be automatically applied by analogy to the interpretation of the agreement. The court here echoed its old decision in *Polydor Limited and RSO Records Inc v Harlequin Records Shops Limited and Simons Records Limited*, Case 270/80, which concerned the free trade agreement between the European Economic Community and Portugal (prior to Portuguese accession) (Official Journal of the European Communities, 1982). The court here decided that identical provisions in the agreement to the treaty provisions on the free movement of goods could not be interpreted in the same way, because the free trade agreement did 'not have the same purpose as the EEC Treaty, inasmuch as the latter, as has been stated above, seeks to create a single market reproducing as closely as possible the conditions of a domestic market'.

In a subsequent case on the Swiss agreements, Case C-541/08 *Fokus Invest*, the question was whether a company established in Austria, but with Swiss owners, could be discriminated against regarding the right to acquire and register immovable property. In this case the court found that the requirement of equal treatment in the agreement applied only to natural persons, and the general prohibition against discrimination on the ground of nationality could not be applied (Official Journal of the European Union, 2010). The answer was therefore yes, Austrian law could discriminate against a company established in Austria with Swiss owners. These cases are clear illustrations of the fact that, regardless of the intent of the parties and the wording of their agreement, it is up to the Court of Justice to establish the nature of the association that is ensured by the agreement.

Concluding reflections

In this chapter, we have provided a brief overview of the EU's range of affiliations with non-members in order to place the EEA Agreement and Norway's other EU affiliations, which we discuss in detail in the next chapter, in a broader perspective. Differences in affiliations are not only about the political priorities that states have, but also reflect degrees of congruence between the EU and its surroundings. Those states that seek to become EU members must go through a comprehensive vetting process in order to demonstrate that they will be able to function as full-fledged EU members. That substantially narrows the range of relevant associations for an EU ex-member. The most relevant group of states to draw lessons from for the UK are those states that qualify for EU membership but for various reasons have decided not to become EU members. Out of these, the two most relevant ones are Switzerland and Norway.

Analysts have examined whether the unique Swiss form of sectoral bilateralism provides Switzerland with more scope for retaining state and popular sovereignty in return for a weaker form of market access than is the case with the multilateral EEA. As will be readily apparent when considering the EEA Agreement in the next chapter, the scope of the Swiss EU affiliation is less comprehensive than the EEA and covers much less of the country's economic and social activities. In addition, the relationship between the EU and Switzerland is less hierarchical, since there is no set of supranational arrangements that regulates it. Analysts have, however, noted that 'Swiss bilateralism – while apparently more tailored – does not necessarily imply that the EU exerts less influence on Swiss policies [than] ... in the formally more constraining

EEA' (Lavenex and Schwok, 2015, 49). There are significant functionalist pressures that emanate from close patterns of interdependence. The Swiss–EU relationship, it has been shown, is quite dynamic (Vahl and Grolimund, 2006).

Ciarán Burke, Ólafur Ísberg Hannesson and Kristin Bangsund (2016) compare the EEA solution to the Swiss free trade model from a British perspective.[13] Their conclusion is that the Swiss model would entail a measure of uncertainty that could be avoided by opting for an EEA solution. The EEA solution, however, has its own challenges that require a strong political will to overcome. We will highlight some of these challenges. In this respect, the legal challenges related to the sovereignty of the EFTA states are significant. The important catchword here is 'dynamic homogeneity'. For the internal market to function, it must provide for common rules and equal conditions of competition, and equal and adequate means of enforcement. The agreement must achieve this not only at the time of its signature, but in a sustainable way over time. The EEA Agreement shows how this can be achieved without creating a supranational framework, as in the EU.

3

What is the Norway model?

Norway is associated with the EU through more than 130 agreements, ranging from the internal market, Schengen association agreements, agreements on asylum and police cooperation (Dublin I, II and III), agreements on foreign and security policy (Norway participates in the EU's battle groups), agreements on internal security and justice, fisheries, agriculture, to mention a few (see Appendix I). Through these agreements, Norway has incorporated roughly three-quarters of EU legislation compared to those EU member states that have incorporated everything (NOU 2012:2, 3). Key areas that fall outside the scope of the cooperation are the euro, the customs union and foreign trade policy, the Common Agricultural Policy and taxation. Even some of these areas are affected by the rules of the single market. Free movement of capital affects taxation rules, and a substantial number of veterinary and food safety rules are included in the agreement.

The EEA Agreement is beyond doubt the main feature of the Norway model. In contrast to Switzerland's (wide range of) sectoral bilateral agreements, the EEA Agreement is a broad and dynamic multilateral agreement between the (currently) 28 EU member states and the three EFTA states of Iceland,

Liechtenstein and Norway. The EEA brings together the EU member states and the three EFTA states in a single market based on the internal market of the EU. It should be noted that the UK was one of the main initiators of EFTA in 1960, and left EFTA when it joined the EU in 1972.

Within the scope of the EEA Agreement, the rules of the internal market extend to the whole EEA, with the result that people, services, goods and capital can move freely. The EEA Agreement guarantees equal rights and obligations within the internal market for citizens and economic operators in the EEA. The EEA is, however, not a supranational legal order, and contrary to the EU member states, the EFTA states retain, formally speaking, their legislative and judicial sovereignty. The EEA is limited in scope compared to the cooperation within the EU, and does not include such areas as agriculture and fisheries, the Monetary Union or justice and home affairs, to list some of the differences. In addition to the rules of the single market, the agreement also includes other areas such as research and development, education, social policy, the environment, consumer protection, tourism and culture – collectively known as 'flanking and horizontal' policies.

The agreement is based on a two-pillar structure with bridging arrangements between EFTA and the EU (see EFTA, 2017). The institutional arrangement reflects the fact that the EEA-EFTA states were not willing to rescind sovereignty to a set of international institutions, even if, as we shall see, they are profoundly affected by the pooling and sharing that is taking place in the EU.

The purpose of this chapter is to clarify the nature of Norway's relationship to the EU, which can be described as EEA++. We provide an overview of the totality of the arrangement, with an emphasis on spelling out the substantive scope of the arrangements and the manner in which this is organised or structured, in formal terms. We also explain the relationship between the EEA and EFTA. The range of different agreements

Norway has with the EU operate according to different dynamics and decision rules (the EEA versus Schengen are cases in point). We discuss the extent to which the rules and norms are directly applicable to Norway. Formally speaking there is no direct effect, but is formal status consistent with actual practice? We focus on the process of rule and norm adaptation, through parliamentary and administrative procedures.

We have divided the chapter into two main sections. In the first, we spell out the nature of the EEA Agreement, including the institutional apparatus, with emphasis on the main institutions involved, namely the EEA Council, the EEA Committee, the EFTA Court and the EFTA Surveillance Authority (ESA), which monitors compliance with EEA rules in Iceland, Lichtenstein and Norway.

In the second section, the chapter spells out the other arrangements that Norway has with the EU, in the areas of justice and home affairs (Schengen, Dublin I, II, III) and foreign and security policy.

An important purpose is to render explicit what is meant by *dynamic homogeneity* in relation to the EEA Agreement and how that is squared in relation to sovereignty. The discussion in the next chapter is particularly concerned with the legal considerations involved in this.

The EEA Agreement

Background to the agreement

The EEA is an agreement under international public law. With some exceptions, it does not transfer sovereign powers to supranational bodies (the main exceptions are the powers of ESA and the Commission in competition law cases, and powers to the European Authority in aviation safety and to the European Agency for Safety and Health at Work under the European Regulation *on* Registration, Evaluation, Authorisation and

Restriction of Chemicals (REACH) regulation). It comprises a main part, 22 annexes and 49 protocols, and a final act, in addition to decisions adopted by the Joint Committee of the EEA and by the EEA Council. The EEA includes institutions set up by the EFTA states to ensure an independent surveillance authority, as well as to create procedures similar to those existing in the EU – including procedures for ensuring the fulfilment of the obligations under the EEA Agreement and for control of the legality of acts of the EFTA Surveillance Authority regarding competition. The Surveillance and Court Agreement (SCA) between the EFTA states regulates this.

The completion of the internal market in the European Community by the Single European Act in 1986 awoke fear in the EFTA states that they would be subject to new barriers of trade between the Community and EFTA (Børde, 1997). The negotiations that had been held since 1984 to create a 'dynamic European Space' demonstrated that it would not be possible to create equal treatment for operators from the EFTA countries in the internal market of the EU by taking over rules for particular sectors only. 'The development showed that, precisely as within a national legal system, legislation in one field of EC law is often dependent upon legislation in other neighbouring fields in order to be applied efficiently' (Nordberg and Johansson, 2016, 20). A more comprehensive approach was therefore needed.

The EEA Agreement was signed on 17 March 1993 between the EU and its member states on the one side, and the EFTA states – Austria, Finland, Iceland, Norway, Sweden and Switzerland – on the other. At the time, the EFTA states were linked to the European Community through almost identical free trade agreements in industrial goods, and constituted the EU's largest market – larger than the USA and Japan combined.[14] The agreement was 'designed as a medium-speed alternative for seven countries on the outskirts of Western Europe, which for various reasons could not or would not contemplate full membership' in the EU (Sejersted, 1997, 44).

Within the EEA, the EU's legislation – in contrast to the situation in the member states – is not formally anchored in the legal precepts of supremacy and direct effect. The reality is, however, not as different as the formal structure would suggest. In the member states, EU law trumps national law in those issue areas where the EU has been conferred competence. In Norway, ESA ensures that legal incorporation is in accordance with EU law, and the EFTA Court in practice ensures the incorporation of EU law. This relationship is clearly one-way; Norwegian citizens are pure recipients of decisions made outside of Norway. There is no form of reciprocity or 'export' of Norwegian decisions to the EU. The Norwegian process of incorporating legislation starts *after* a decision has been reached in the EU. Through Norway's dense relationship with the EU, Norway is not only subject to far more legislation from the EU than from any other international organisation; it is a recipient of legal norms from a system with obvious constitutional features, however that system is defined. Some claim that the Norwegian popularly elected representatives and the Norwegian government have lost the right of initiative as per Article 76 of the Norwegian constitution (Stavang, 2002, 135). Others have characterised the EEA Agreement as locating its members in a 'semi-colonial' setting (Tovias, 2006). The predominant position in Norwegian constitutional law is nevertheless that the EEA Agreement basically is within the constitution, and it has broad support among the politicians and the population of Norway.

Overview over the EEA Agreement

The EEA Agreement came into effect in 1994 (for Lichtenstein it took effect on 1 May 1995). It is based on a two-pillar structure with bridging institutions, and includes a court and a surveillance body. The two-pillar structure was seen as the only possible solution to ensure that the agreement remained an intergovernmental agreement without supranational characteristics (Børde, 1997, 11). The EEA countries are not part of the EU's customs union. When the EEA Agreement took effect, the EEA countries had to incorporate all relevant EU legislation that was in effect at the time of signing the agreement. In line with what was said about EU conditionality above, the EEA Agreement is intended to ensure legal homogeneity within the entire 31-member EEA. The EEA Agreement is therefore a dynamic agreement: new relevant EU legislation is incorporated in an ongoing manner albeit subject to specific decision procedures.

The main objective of the EEA Agreement is to establish:

a dynamic and homogeneous European Economic Area, based on common rules and equal conditions of competition and providing for the adequate means of enforcement including at the judicial level, and achieved on the basis of equality and reciprocity and of an overall balance of benefits, rights and obligations for the Contracting Parties. (Official Journal of the European Communities, 1994b)

This expresses the determination of the contracting parties to provide for the fullest possible realisation of the free movement of goods, persons, services and capital within the whole European Economic Area, as well as for strengthened and broadened cooperation in flanking and horizontal policies. The agreement emphasises the important role that individuals will play in the European Economic Area through the exercise of the rights conferred on them by this agreement and through the judicial defence of these rights.

The agreement consists of a main part, with 129 articles in nine parts, 49 protocols and 22 annexes. The EEA Agreement includes all the market freedoms of the single market unless otherwise explicitly stated. The main part of the agreement contains the basic provisions on free movement of goods (part two), free movement of persons, services and capital (part three), competition and other common rules (part four) and horizontal provisions relevant to the four freedoms (part five). Part seven gives the institutional provisions, part eight the financial mechanism and part nine the general and final provisions. The main bulk of harmonised legislation is contained in the annexes. Currently, more than 11,000 EU acts have been incorporated into the agreement since the signing in 1992, mainly through updating the acts included in the annexes. The main part of the agreement is unchanged in substance since 1992, but has been amended to reflect the various enlargements of the EU.

A substantial part of the EEA Agreement concerns the free movement of goods. The main principle emanating from the agreement is that products may be traded between all 31 EEA states without customs duties or hindrance from national regulations. This does not extend to all goods. Following Article 8 (3) (a) and (b) of the EEA Agreement, only products falling under certain chapters of the Harmonized Commodity Description and Coding System, as well as products specified in Protocol 3 to the EEA Agreement, are subject to the principle of free movement of goods (Official Journal of the European Communities, 1994b). The most important exceptions are those for agricultural products and fisheries, which apply for the whole of the agreement. Since the EEA is not a customs union, the provisions on free movement of goods only apply to goods originating in the EEA unless otherwise explicitly stated. Free movement of persons is also not without exceptions. Lichtenstein has an option to place quantitative restrictions on the number of new residents. EEA citizens may move freely into Lichtenstein, but need to apply for a permit if they wish to reside there.

In addition to the market freedoms, the agreement includes rules on competition and state aid, and closer cooperation in other fields, such as research and development, the environment, education and social policy. These are the so-called 'horizontal provisions related to the four freedoms' and 'cooperation outside of the four freedoms'. Here we find the harmonised rules of the EU that protect legitimate interests, for example health, safety, consumer interests and the environment, that goods and services must adhere to in order to move freely within the internal market. We also find rules on common policies such as research, development and higher education.

In addition to rules that apply to specific issues, the agreement includes some general, overarching principles. The most important of these are the prohibition against discrimination on grounds of nationality in Article 4, and the principle of loyalty in Article 3. Article 3 states that:

> The Contracting Parties shall take all appropriate measures, whether general or particular, to ensure fulfilment of the obligations arising out of this Agreement. They shall abstain from any measure which could jeopardize the attainment of the objectives of this Agreement. Moreover, they shall facilitate cooperation within the framework of this Agreement. (Official Journal of the European Communities, 1994a)

As in EU law, this has been interpreted as being directed to all bodies within the contracting parties, including the courts. From this principle therefore flows also the principle that national law should be interpreted in conformity with EEA rules, as far as that is possible within the recognised method of interpretation.

It is one thing to state the intention of arriving at and maintaining a uniform interpretation of the rules, 'in full deference to the independence of the courts'. To establish the institutional structure for it and to ensure it in practice is, however, another matter. The first attempt of the contracting parties was flouted by the European Court of Justice (ECJ). In its opinion 1/91, the court rejected the proposed EEA Court, because the proposal conferred matters of interpretation of Community law to a body outside of the EU treaties (Official Journal of the European Communities, 1991).[15]

The court underlined in paragraph 14 that the fact that 'the provisions of the agreement and the corresponding Community provisions are identically worded does not mean that they must necessarily be interpreted identically', because an 'international treaty is to be interpreted not only on the basis of its wording, but also in light of its objectives' (Official Journal of the European Communities, 1991). The court referred to its interpretation of the free trade agreement with Portugal, where it declined to interpret a provision worded identically to the provision of the treaty on the free movement of goods in line with its case law on this provision (Official Journal of the European Communities, 1982). The court stressed in paragraph 16 of the Portugal ruling that 'the Treaty, by establishing a common market and progressively approximating the economic policies of the Member States, seeks to unite national markets into a single market having the characteristics of a domestic market' (Official Journal of the European Communities, 1982). In its 1991 opinion, paragraph 16, the court said that the rules on free trade in the Community have 'developed and form part of the community legal order, the objectives of which go beyond that of the agreement' and are thus not ends in themselves, but are means of achieving European integration (Official Journal of the European Communities, 1991). Community law is therefore inherently different from provisions of a free trade agreement.

The result of this opinion was that the agreement was renegotiated. Instead of an EEA court, the EFTA parties agreed to set up parallel institutions in the SCA, thus establishing the EFTA Court. The EFTA Court is an independent court, but is bound to the jurisprudence of the CJEU by Article 3 of the SCA. Article 3 (2) states:

In the interpretation and application of the EEA Agreement and this Agreement, the EFTA Surveillance Authority and the EFTA Court shall pay due account to the principles laid down by the relevant rulings by the Court of Justice of the European Communities given after the date of signature of the EEA Agreement and which concern the interpretation of that Agreement or of such rules of the Treaty establishing the European Economic Community and the Treaty establishing the European Coal and Steel Community in so far as they are identical in substance to the provisions of the EEA Agreement or to the provisions of Protocols 1 to 4 and the provisions of the acts corresponding to those listed in Annexes I and II to the present Agreement. (Official Journal of the European Communities, 1994a, Article 3 (2))

The arrangements set up in the EEA Agreement have been successful. In its judgment in case C-452/01 *Ospelt*, the CJEU stated:

one of the principal aims of the EEA Agreement is to provide for the fullest possible realisation of the free movement of goods, persons, services and capital within the whole European Economic Area, so that the internal market established within the European Union is extended to the EFTA States. From that angle, several provisions of the abovementioned Agreement are intended to ensure as uniform an interpretation as possible thereof throughout the EEA (see Opinion 1/92 [1992] ECR I-2821). It is for the Court, in that context, to ensure that the rules of the EEA Agreement which are identical in substance to those of the Treaty are interpreted uniformly within the Member States. (Official Journal of the European Communities, 2003)

The EFTA Court has also seen it as an overriding aim to arrive at uniform interpretations, except for instances where differences in interpretation are merited by differences in the rules or aims between the EEA and EU law (see Baudenbacher, 2005, 48).

An important purpose of the EEA Agreement is also to conserve legal homogeneity within the entire EEA. For this purpose, the agreement is *dynamic*, in depth and breadth terms: new relevant legislation is included in an ongoing manner. The agreement is territorially expanded in line with every expansion in EU membership. The application of the rules under the agreement also develops with treaty revisions within the EU. This set of agreements gives the EEA states assured access to the EU's internal market and locates them within the EU's borders with responsibility for border control.

An important part of the EEA is its institutional arrangements. The main operative institution is the EEA Joint Committee. The committee shall ensure the effective implementation and operation of this agreement, see Article 92 (1) (Official Journal of the European Communities, 1994b). It consists of representatives of the contracting parties, and takes decisions by agreement between the Community, represented by the Commission, on the one hand, and the EFTA states 'speaking with one voice' on the other. This means that all the EFTA states must agree in order for a decision to be taken. In popular terms, this is often referred to as a right for each EFTA state to veto regarding the inclusion of new EU laws in the agreement. We see, however, that a veto by one state entails a veto for all. This is therefore not an 'opt-out' clause that EFTA states may exercise for their own part.

The agreement also states, in Article 108, that the EFTA states shall establish an independent surveillance authority and a court of justice. They shall also establish procedures similar to those existing in the Community, including procedures for ensuring the fulfilment of obligations under this agreement and for control of the legality of acts of the ESA regarding competition.

Article 109 (2) states that to ensure a uniform surveillance throughout the EEA, the EFTA Surveillance Authority and the EC Commission shall cooperate, exchange information and consult each other on surveillance policy issues and individual cases (Official Journal of the European Communities, 1994b). In case of disagreement between these two bodies with regard to the action to be taken in relation to a complaint or with regard to the result of the examination, either of the bodies may refer the matter to the EEA Joint Committee. The EFTA Court shall be competent, in particular, for actions regarding the surveillance procedure by ESA, appeals concerning decisions by ESA in the field of competition and the settlement of disputes between the EFTA states.

The surveillance authority and the EFTA Court are established in the agreement between the EFTA states on the establishment of a surveillance authority and a Court of Justice. The EU is not party to this agreement. Part two and three of this agreement establishes the ESA, part four the court. In addition to the competences stipulated in the EEA Agreement, the SCA establishes for the EFTA states the equivalent to the preliminary ruling procedure in the EU. Article 34 states that where a question on the interpretation of the EEA Agreement is raised before any court or tribunal in an EFTA state, that court or tribunal may, if it considers it necessary to enable it to give judgment, request the EFTA Court to give an opinion on this (Official Journal of the European Communities, 1994a). In such cases, the jurisdiction of the EFTA Court is to give an 'advisory opinion'. This distinguishes these proceedings from the proceedings on preliminary rulings within the EU, where the rulings of the court are *binding* on the national court. Another difference is that there is *no express obligation* on a national court of last instance to refer matters to the EFTA Court. The national courts of the EFTA states are 'EEA courts' on equal footing with the EFTA Court and the CJEU.

Related to the EEA Agreement are the EEA Grants. These provide social and economic development funding from the EEA-EFTA states. This financial support aims at reducing economic and social disparities in the EEA and strengthening bilateral relations with the beneficiary states: Bulgaria, Cyprus, Czech Republic, Estonia, Greece, Hungary, Latvia, Lithuania, Malta, Poland, Portugal, Romania, Slovakia, Slovenia and Spain. In addition to the EEA Grants, Norway has funded a parallel scheme since 2004 – the Norway Grants.

Affiliations beyond the EEA Agreement

As mentioned above, the relationship between Norway and the EU is governed by more than 75 agreements in addition to the EEA Agreement. More than 50 of these were concluded after the EEA Agreement entered into force (NOU 2012:2, 115). The agreements between Norway and the EU have been characterised as patchwork, with no internal structure and with inconsistent institutional frameworks (NOU 2012:2, 14). If we look more closely at Norway, we see that it has signed a number of additional parallel agreements with the EU, including agreements on asylum and police cooperation (Dublin I, II and III) and on foreign and security policy – Norwegian troops are at the disposal of the EU's battle groups. In formal terms there are no connections between the EEA agreements and the other agreements between Norway and the EU.

Although technically part of the EEA Agreement, the agreement on veterinary issues could be mentioned here. The agreement was concluded between the EU and the EFTA countries in 1998, and was adopted into the EEA Agreement through a replacement of its Annex 1. Over time it has grown into the largest component of the EEA, comprising over 40% of all its legislation (NOU 2012:2, 16). The veterinary legislation covers animal and public health requirements for the production, trade and imports of live animals and animal products, as well as issues related to the control of these products. Arrangements for animal welfare and the control and prevention of animal diseases are also included. All sectors of the food chain are covered, including feed production, primary production, processing, storage, transport and sale to the consumer. In the period 2002–2004, the EU adopted legislation concerning general food law and the European Food Safety Authority, as well as legislation concerning hygiene and control in the food production chain and legislation concerning animal by-products. The Food Law Package entered into force in the EEA on 1 May 2010. With the implementation of the Food Law Package, the essential food law is now harmonised within the EEA. In addition, the EFTA states are ensured participation in the European Food Safety Authority (EFSA).

An important agreement outside the EEA is the Schengen Association Agreement. The agreement was signed in 1999 and entered into force in 2001 (Official Journal of the European Communities, 1999). An open market in goods, services, persons and capital requires low-threshold access and passage. That is one of the reasons why the EEA-EFTA states have signed Schengen association agreements, which in effect locates them within the EU's external borders and systems of border controls.

The Schengen cooperation was originally established in 1985 between Belgium, the Netherlands, Luxembourg, France and Germany. When the Nordic EU members – Denmark, Sweden and Finland – applied to join the Schengen cooperation, Norway and Iceland also had to enter into a cooperation agreement with the Schengen countries so that the Nordic Passport Union could be retained. This agreement was signed on 19 December 1996. When the provisions in the Amsterdam Treaty integrated the Schengen cooperation into the EU, a new institutional framework was needed, and the Schengen Association Agreement between Norway, Iceland and the EU had to be concluded. A similar agreement has been concluded with Switzerland and Lichtenstein.

The agreement on participation in the Schengen cooperation gives Norway and Iceland the right and the obligation to apply all the Schengen rules. In the same way as in the EEA, the association agreement consists of a main part and a large body of rules of secondary legislation constituting the Schengen *acquis*. The *acquis* is dynamic and develops by changes in the EU legislation that is included in the association agreement. When developing new rules, the European Commission is obliged to consult experts from Norway and Iceland in the same way that it consults experts from the EU countries. The Schengen rules cover several areas, namely rules on checks on persons at the outer borders, harmonisation of the conditions of entry and of the rules on visas for short stays (up to three months), enhanced police cooperation (including rights of cross-border surveillance and hot pursuit), and stronger judicial cooperation on criminal cases through a faster extradition system and transfer of enforcement of criminal judgments on police cooperation. In addition, the agreement includes the establishment and development of the Schengen Information System (SIS). The SIS is a large-scale information system that supports external border control and law enforcement cooperation in the Schengen states. The United Kingdom also operates the SIS but, as it has chosen not to join the Schengen area, the UK cannot issue or access Schengen-wide alerts for refusing entry into or stay in the Schengen area.

Schengen has its own institutional arrangements that differ from those of the EEA. The main institution is the Mixed Committee, which is made up of the EU member states, the European Commission and the four associated countries: Norway, Iceland, Switzerland and Liechtenstein. All Schengen-relevant issues that arise in the ongoing cooperation are discussed in this committee. Moreover, whenever the European Council is developing rules that do not fall within the scope of the agreement but can nevertheless be of significance for the cooperation, the Mixed Committee must be informed. Once proposals for new rules have been discussed in the Mixed

Committee, the rules may be adopted by the EU member states in the European Council. The EFTA countries then decide on an independent basis whether to adopt these rules and incorporate them into national law. There is therefore no common decision-making body as within the EEA. The agreement has a cliff-edge clause: should either Iceland or Norway decide not to adopt new Schengen legislation that has been enacted in the EU, the agreement shall be considered terminated with respect to Iceland or Norway, as the case may be, unless the Mixed Committee, after a careful examination of ways to continue the agreement, decides otherwise within 90 days (Official Journal of the European Communities, 1999, Article 8 (4)).

There is no Schengen Court, and the EFTA Court is not empowered to deal with issues that arise under the Schengen agreements. Article 9 of the Association Agreement states that in order to achieve the objective of the contracting parties to arrive at as uniform an application and interpretation as possible of the provisions of the Schengen *acquis*, the Mixed Committee shall keep under constant review the development of the case law of the Court of Justice of the European Communities, as well as the development of the case law of the competent courts of Iceland and Norway relating to such provisions (Official Journal of the European Communities, 1999). Iceland and Norway are entitled to submit statements of case or written observations to the Court of Justice in cases where a question has been referred to it by a court or tribunal of a member state for a preliminary ruling concerning the interpretation of any provision on Schengen. In the case a of substantial difference in application between the authorities of the member states concerned and those of Iceland or Norway in respect of the provisions, the Mixed Committee shall try to settle the dispute within 90 days. If this fails, after a further period of 30 days the agreement shall, according to Article 11, be considered terminated. The termination takes effect after six months (Official Journal of the European Communities, 1999).

The Schengen cooperation covers a clearly limited area within the EU cooperation on justice and home affairs. There are many other areas where Norway and the EU have common challenges and interests, as well as a mutual desire for cooperation. There are therefore a number of other association agreements between Norway and the EU. One of the most important of these is the agreement entered into in 2001 on Norwegian participation in the Dublin *acquis*, the agreement between the European Community and Iceland and Norway concerning the criteria and mechanisms for establishing the state responsible for examining a request for asylum lodged in a member state or in Iceland or Norway (Official Journal of the European Communities, 2001). The agreement refers to the Schengen Agreement, and states that the application and development of the Schengen *acquis* calls for the conclusion of an appropriate arrangement on the criteria and mechanisms for establishing the state responsible for examining a request for asylum lodged in any of the member states or in Iceland and Norway (Official Journal of the European Communities, 2001, Article 1).

The agreement states that the main provisions of the Dublin Convention (now the Dublin III regulation), as well as relevant decisions of the committee established pursuant to Article 18 of the Dublin Convention shall be implemented by Iceland and Norway and applied in their mutual relations and in their relations with the member states (Official Journal of the European Communities, 2001). It also obliges Norway and Iceland to implement and apply the provisions of the Data Protection Directive. The agreement applies to the provisions of the regulation concerning the establishment of 'Eurodac' for the comparison of the fingerprints of applicants for asylum and certain other third-country nationals to facilitate the implementation of the Dublin regulation.

The institutional arrangements that are established are similar to those of the Schengen Association Agreement. The agreement establishes a joint committee. When drafting new legislation, the Commission shall informally seek advice from experts of Iceland and Norway in the same way it seeks advice from experts of the member states for drawing up its proposals. During the phase preceding the adoption of legislation, the contracting parties consult each other again in the Joint Committee at significant moments at the request of one of them. Decisions on new acts or measures are not taken in the Joint Committee, but in the Dublin Committee and by Norway and Iceland respectively. The same cliff-edge clause applies: the agreement is suspended if Norway or Iceland fails to adopt new acts or measures.

Other parts of EU justice and home affairs cooperation also have implications for Norway. Therefore, Norway and the EU have agreed cooperation within various areas, including the following:

- The European Migration Network, which contributes to policy development on migration and asylum;
- the European Asylum Support Office (EASO), which aims at enhancing practical cooperation on asylum matters and helping member states fulfil their European and international obligations to give protection to people in need;
- EUROPOL, the European Law Enforcement Organisation, which aims at improving cooperation between the competent authorities in EU member states and their effectiveness in preventing and combating terrorism, drug trafficking and other forms of organised crime. Norwegian liaison officers are posted to the organisation's headquarters in The Hague;
- EUROJUST, a cooperation network set up to encourage and coordinate the investigation and prosecution of serious cross-border crime. Norwegian public prosecutors and police prosecutors work for EUROJUST in The Hague;
- an agreement on mutual legal assistance (exchange of information between law enforcement and prosecution services);

- association to the European Arrest Warrant system, which provides a mechanism for the surrender of individuals suspected or convicted of crimes between European countries;
- an agreement on the Prüm Treaty on enhanced police cooperation in order to combat terrorism and international crime;
- Norway has concluded negotiations on association to the European Agency for the operational management of large-scale IT systems in the area of freedom, security and justice (EU-LISA), the IT agency managing all large-scale IT systems within the justice and home affairs area.

According to Article 83 TFEU, the European Parliament and the Council may establish minimum rules concerning the definition of criminal offences and sanctions in the areas of particularly serious crime with a cross-border dimension (Official Journal of the European Union, 2012). The areas of crime included are terrorism, trafficking in human beings and sexual exploitation of women and children, illicit drug trafficking, illicit arms trafficking, money laundering, corruption, counterfeiting of means of payment, computer crime and organised crime. Norway is not formally tied to this. Nevertheless, Norway has adapted its criminal law in several instances to coordinate with the EU definitions and sanctions, particularly in the definitions of corruption and terrorism. In reforms of the legislation on trafficking and child pornography the EU legislation has been taken into account.

There are also agreements between the EU and Norway in the area of defence and security. Norway contributes significantly to the Common Security and Defence Policy, and takes part in activities directly linked to the areas of responsibility of the European Defence Agency (EDA). Norway participated in the European Union Police Mission (EUPM) in Bosnia and Herzegovina in 2002 and the EU and Norway have subsequently concluded an agreement on the participation of the Kingdom of Norway in the crisis management operations led by the European Union. Norway participates in 7 out of the EU's 15 capability development groups (EUCAP): Intelligence, surveillance, target acquisition, and reconnaissance (ISTAR), robot and Unmanned Aerial Vehicle (UAV), Space Assets, Strategic Sealift, Strategic Airlift, Air-to-Air Refuelling, and nuclear, biological, chemical (NBC). Most of these groups coordinate their efforts with identical or similar North Atlantic Treaty Organization (NATO) groups. Norway and the EDA agreed on administrative arrangements in 2006 enabling Norway to participate in EDA's projects and programmes. The agreement was the result of intense diplomatic efforts from the Norwegian side, and Norway was seriously disappointed over the fact that it did not achieve full membership in the agency (Sjursen, 2014, 183). A consultative committee provides a forum for exchanging views and information on matters of common interest. A point of contact has been established on the agency's staff and the Norwegian Ministry of Defence has designated a liaison officer at Norway's mission to the EU. Norway plays an active role in armaments-related cooperation, currently taking place within the Western European Armament Group (WEAG) and the Western European Armament Organisation (WEAO). Norway is also a substantial contributor to the research and technology cooperation under WEAG.

Concluding reflections

This chapter has provided an overview of the various components of the so-called Norway model. This model, as we have shown, cannot be boiled down to the single market or the EEA Agreement, but includes a wide range of (more than 75) agreements in addition to the EEA. It reflects the fact that Norway seeks as close a cooperation as possible with the EU without becoming an EU member. At the same time, the

Norway model reflects the complex nature of the EU, and the difficulties facing non-members in aligning with the EU over time. For instance, Norway has been developing a number of cooperations specific to the Common Foreign and Security Policy and Justice and Home Affairs (the Maastricht pillars), just as the Union itself has sought to make those forms of cooperation less distinct from the rest of EU's decision making. Thus, somewhat ironically, the EU's Maastricht pillars are more pronounced in the Norway model than in the present-day EU, because some of the elements of the Norway model retain a stronger pillar imprint than is the case within the EU (Schengen is a case in point; see Fredriksen, 2015).

In the Norway model, the core notion of dynamic homogeneity appears as a three-pronged phenomenon: first to ensure homogeneity between the three EFTA states and the EU members; second to ensure homogeneity with new EU members, as a consequence of EU enlargements; and third to ensure homogeneity across policy areas, in line with the expanded functional reach of the single market. The first two of these homogenising processes have largely operated in sync; less so the third, since the EEA is functionally different from the EU (agriculture and fisheries).

The objectives underpinning the EEA are different from those of the EU, in the sense that the former is not imbued with the goal of ensuring 'ever closer union'. Since an international treaty is to be interpreted not only on the basis of its wording, but also in light of its objectives, diverging interpretations may arise.

These points of convergence and divergence underline the need to take a closer look at how the three considerations of market and other forms of assured access are balanced in relation to sovereign state and democratic control. That is the topic of the next two chapters.

4

The challenge of sovereignty

This chapter focuses on the elusive concept of sovereignty. Sovereignty is more aptly conceived of as a normative term than as a factual description of any given state of affairs. It is common to distinguish between state and popular sovereignty. The former is embedded in the law of the peoples, whereas the latter has references to the UN Convention on Human Rights and democratic constitutions. In today's interdependent world, the states' ability to assert sovereignty as independence is greatly curtailed. Many sovereign decisions are dictated by the force of necessity, such as when globalisation forces a country to change its tax regime to attract investments. Even when the need to take action is imposed by another country, we do not necessarily say that the country facing the imposition lacks sovereignty. When the US imposes special security requirements on travellers to the country, other countries have had to adapt or close their airports for travel to the US. Traditionally dominant countries like the UK may have other experiences and attitudes to external constraints than traditionally less influential countries like Norway, but from the point of view of sovereignty their situation in relation to globalisation is the same.

In the following, we approach the assessment of sovereignty from a legal perspective. There is a large body of literature on sovereignty from a political science perspective, which either treats it as a normative – regulatory - term or focuses on the aspect of power, which brings it closer to autonomy and the actual ability to rule oneself. We will address these dimensions in the next chapter. This chapter provides a legal reading of sovereignty in relation to the Norway model.

A state may undertake obligations under public international law without giving up any part of its sovereignty. It is not even necessary that the state has voluntarily agreed to undertake the obligation. Customary international law is binding even on sovereign states. What does raise problems is when other institutions than organs of the state have power to enact or enforce obligations within the state. Sovereignty can thus be defined as the exclusive power of state organs to take decisions with binding effect within the state.

Based on the basic powers of a state, we can distinguish between legislative, judicial and executive sovereignty. Legislative sovereignty is challenged when an organ outside of the state is empowered to legislate within the state, such as when the EU has the power to enact regulations that are binding in their entirety and are directly applicable in all European Union countries (Official Journal of the European Union, 2012, Article 288). Judicial sovereignty is challenged when an external court such as the CJEU gives rulings that are binding for national courts in dealing with specific cases. Executive sovereignty is challenged when an external body such as the Commission passes decisions that are binding on legal bodies within the state, as they do in competition cases. In all these respects, EU law goes beyond international law and is therefore characterised as supranational.

Approaching the challenge of dynamic homogeneity

The basic aim in constructing the EEA Agreement was to achieve participation of the EFTA countries in the internal market of the EU without a supranational construction requiring the EFTA states to cede sovereignty in the legal sense. Setting up an arrangement with rules in the EEA identical to those in the EU at the time of the agreement was one thing, ensuring *dynamic* homogeneity quite another.[16] There were two basic challenges in achieving dynamic homogeneity. The first was to ensure equal application of the rules within the EU and the EFTA pillars as time passed – the dynamic aspect of already agreed rules. The particular challenges here were a combination of the fact that EU law develops through a dynamic interpretation by the Court of Justice, based on a teleological approach to the rules, with the maintenance of the judicial and legislative sovereignty of the EFTA states. The second was to have a mechanism for including new legislation in the EEA as the *acquis* develops through adoption of new legislation in the EU. An unforeseen challenge was also the degree to which EU law changes through treaty revisions and the adoption of completely new concepts through new treaties, such as EU citizenship, foreign and security policy, justice and home affairs and fundamental rights.

Some mechanisms of dynamic homogeneity were built into the agreement itself. Recital 4 of the preamble to the agreement proclaims that the EEA is 'based on common rules and equal conditions of competition and providing for the adequate means of enforcement including at the judicial level, and achieved on the basis of equality and reciprocity and of an overall balance of benefits, rights and obligations for the Contracting Parties' (Official Journal of the European Communities, 1994b). Recital 15 of the preamble states the objective of the contracting parties 'to arrive at, and maintain, a uniform interpretation and application of this Agreement and those provisions of Community legislation which are substantially reproduced in this Agreement and to arrive at an equal treatment of individuals and economic operators as regards the four freedoms and the conditions of competition' (Official Journal of the European Communities, 1994b). Of note is also Recital 8, which underlines 'the important role that individuals will play in the European Economic Area through the exercise of the rights conferred on them by this Agreement and through the judicial defence of these rights' (Official Journal of the European Communities, 1994b). The preamble has been taken to imply that the EEA is a community of rights, based on equal protection of the rights in the EU and the EFTA pillars of the EEA, ensuring equal conditions of competition within the whole EEA.

There are also more specific institutional mechanisms for homogeneity, surveillance procedure and settlement of disputes. Article 3 puts a duty of loyalty on the parties and states that the 'Contracting Parties shall take all appropriate measures, whether general or particular, to ensure fulfilment of the obligations arising out of this Agreement' (Official Journal of the European Communities, 1994b). The principle of loyalty has been used by the EFTA Court to guarantee, in various ways, that EEA law becomes effective law at the national level. The principle affects and strengthens the duty of the EFTA states to make secondary EEA legislation a part of their internal legal order and imposes duties on the national courts of the EFTA states to give full effect to EEA law (Hreinsson, 2015).

In Article 4, there is a general prohibition against discrimination on grounds of nationality. From the development of EU law, we have seen the power that lies in such general provisions on the duty of loyalty and the prohibition against discrimination on grounds of nationality. Protocol 35 of the agreement addresses the issue of supremacy. It obliges the EFTA states to ensure that EEA rules prevail over rules of national law in cases of conflict. Article 7 of the agreement requires EU regulations are made part of the internal legal order of the contracting parties 'as such' and that directives are implemented in the 'form and method, chosen by the Contracting Party' (Official Journal of the European Communities, 1994b).

Legislative sovereignty

One challenge to overcome was the hurdle of legislative sovereignty and, at the same time, achieving reciprocity in the protection of rights in the EU and the EEA. At the outset, reconciling these two aims would seem impossible (see Graver, 2002). Not only were the EFTA states reluctant to enter into an agreement that encroached upon their sovereignty, but the CJEU was sceptical of the EEA Agreement due to its lack of reciprocity (see Fredriksen, 2010). The court emphasised that the EEA Agreement 'only creates rights and obligations between the Contracting Parties, and provides for no transfer of sovereign rights to the inter-governmental institutions which it sets up', whereas the EEC Treaty was heralded as 'the constitutional charter of a Community based on the rule of law' (Official Journal of the European Communities, 1991, paragraph 20). EU law is characterised by EU treaties and legislation having direct effect in the member states with supremacy over national law. In this way, it differs greatly from international public law, where national law determines the extent to which international law is to have effect in the internal legal orders. The EEA Agreement takes as its starting point public international law, but with some important qualifications in the form of explicit duties that the contracting parties have agreed to: for example, including EU legislation in the agreement, and duties to ensure that EEA rules are given effect in national law and the ways in which EU legislation is valid in the member states.

Introduction of new rules

Being an agreement under public international law, no new obligations can be introduced into the EEA without the consent of every contracting party. The EEA Joint Committee takes decisions on the inclusion of new obligations by agreement between the Community, on the one hand, and the EFTA states on the other. In the EEA Joint Committee, the EFTA states are 'speaking with one voice' (Official Journal of the European Communities, 1994b, Article 93 (2)). The effect of this is that they all must agree in order for a new piece of legislation to be included in the agreement. If one of the EFTA states opposes a regulation or a directive, the 'voice' of EFTA is against including it in the agreement. From the EU point of view, decisions of the EEA Joint Committee have the effect that the territorial scope of an EU rule is widened beyond the European Union to the three EFTA states. EU businesses and citizens are thus given the same rights in the three EFTA countries as within the EU, at the price of accepting that businesses and citizens of these three countries have these rights within the EU. On the Community side, Community law governs the decision-making procedure (see Official Journal of the European Communities, 1982). On the EFTA side, national law governs the effect of EEA obligations in their internal legal orders. The agreement, however, does contain some obligations to which the national law of the EFTA states should conform. Whenever the EU adopts a legislative act on an issue that the agreement covers, according to Article 102 the EU should inform the other contracting parties in the EEA Joint Committee as soon as possible. The EEA Joint Committee should make a decision concerning the amendment as close as possible to the adoption by the EU of the corresponding legislation with a view to permitting a simultaneous application in the EU and the EEA. If, at the end of six months, the EEA Joint Committee has not taken a decision, 'the affected part' of the agreement is regarded as provisionally suspended. This is reciprocity in practice: if the EFTA countries do not take on board amendments to harmonise legislation, the harmonisation of rules in this area is put off.

In practice, new EU rules are not formally referred to the EEA Joint Committee before there is agreement, in order to avoid the launch of the time limit and the suspension of common rules in an area while negotiations are taking place. For instance, the Norwegian government at the time did not want to adopt in 2008 the third postal directive that liberalised all postal services. A refusal should have led to the suspension of the two previous directives, with the consequence that there would have been no free movement of any postal services within the EEA. The third directive was not referred to the EEA Joint Committee before there was a change in government in Norway that was willing to adopt it. It was finally adopted in 2015, and free movement was introduced in 2016, four years later than in the EU.

The understanding of reciprocity that is built into Article 102 has the effect that failure to adopt new EU rules in the agreement not only potentially hinders free movement due to lack of harmonisation on these new aspects, but it also entails that whole stocks of harmonised rules unravel. Trade of goods and services in the affected area is then governed by the fall-back position of the main part of the agreement, which is by the treaty provisions alone. Restrictions must be justified, but since there are no harmonised rules, they may or may not prevail, depending on the circumstances. Harmonisation disappears overnight by lack of agreement on a change or modification in the existing harmonisation.

Adoption of the rules into national law

The EEA is not only about including new legislation in the agreement, but also about transposing these rules into the national law of the EFTA states. Protocol 35 is a main rule concerning legislation and the EEA. It states that the agreement does not require a transfer of legislative powers to any institution of the European Economic Area. Common rules in the EEA consequently must be achieved through national procedures. As its sole article, the protocol then states that 'for cases of possible conflicts between implemented EEA rules and other statutory provisions, the EFTA states undertake to introduce, if necessary, a statutory provision to the effect that EEA rules prevail in these cases' (Official Journal of the European Communities, 1994b). This creates an obligation on the EFTA states but does not entail that EEA rules are part of national law without implementation. If a state fails to implement an EEA rule, the EFTA Surveillance Authority may initiate an infringement procedure against that state, and the state may be ordered to implement it by the EFTA Court. There is, however, no direct effect of such rules as within EU law. On the other hand, the state may be liable to compensate any loss incurred by individuals because of the failure to implement EEA rules properly.

In Norway, the EEA Agreement itself is incorporated into Norwegian law by Section 1 of the EEA law, which states that the main part of the agreement is 'valid as Norwegian law' (Official Journal of the European Communities, 1994b). Section 2 states that legislation incorporating Norwegian obligations under the agreement take precedence over other legislation. Executive orders, regulations and other statutory instruments that incorporate such obligations take precedence over other statutory instruments and over legislation of a later date. Article 7 of the EEA Agreement states that regulations shall be incorporated as such, and directives by the form and method of implementation chosen by the legislator (Official Journal of the European Communities, 1994b).

In other words, as long as the EEA Act is not repealed by an express provision of parliament, the main parts of the agreement (that is, the rules corresponding to the EU Treaty) are effective in Norwegian law with supremacy over other rules, save for the constitution. This is the same type of supremacy that the

UK European Union Act grants EU law in the UK. The main difference is that regulations must be incorporated into national law in the EFTA countries, since there is no transfer of legislative power in the EEA. Incorporated EEA law, regulations and directives that have been implemented by legislative acts are effective in the EFTA states with the same supremacy as EU law in the member states.

From the point of view of Norwegian law, this leaves us with three possible categories of relevant EU legislation: EU legislation that is not part of the agreement because it has not yet been included, legislation that is part of the agreement but not correctly implemented into national law, and implemented EEA law. Once a piece of legislation is adopted in the EU, a decision must be taken by the EEA Joint Committee on whether to include it in the EEA Agreement or not. The EFTA has one vote in the EEA Joint Committee, so all the EFTA countries must agree before an act can be included in the EEA Agreement. This has the potential of causing frictions, because one state may block legislation that the other states want to include. Before a decision is taken in the EEA Joint Committee, the legislation is not part of the EEA Agreement, no matter how relevant it is to the agreement. Once it is included in the agreement, it is binding in the EFTA states as a rule of public international law. It is first with the transposition of the legislation into national law that it takes effect in national law. This means that there is no direct effect of regulations or direct effect without national incorporation.[17]

Substitutes for direct effect

The lack of direct effect does not mean that the EEA rule is without legal consequences. The EFTA Court has consistently taken a dynamic approach to the agreement, and has developed mechanisms through its case law that ensure homogeneity and reciprocity with EU law in lieu of supremacy and direct effect (see in detail Fredriksen, 2010). The national courts of the EFTA states have followed suit. The Norwegian Supreme Court decided in the *Finanger* case that there is a strong interpretative obligation under Norwegian law to interpret national law in conformity with international obligations – EEA law, in particular (Norwegian Supreme Court, 2000). The court referred to the case law of the CJEU, and the majority of the court stated that the duty to interpret in accordance with EEA law did not entail a duty to interpret national law *contra legem*. The effect, then, is that non-transposed directives are given a sort of direct effect in Norwegian law, but not supremacy. It could be argued that this was not a necessary consequence of the case but was a question of horizontal effect, and was not recognised even in EU law. There is no doubt today, however, that the result applies also to issues of direct effect in cases against public bodies. This was a long-contested issue in the legal doctrine, until the EFTA Court accepted in 2002 that the EEA Agreement does not entail a doctrine of direct effect independent of national incorporation.[18]

The story does not end here, however. Finanger, who had been seriously injured in a car accident and who claimed compensation under the motor vehicle insurance directives, subsequently filed a case against the government for damages, since the lack of implementation of the directives in Norwegian law deprived her of her insurance.

The EFTA Court had already advised, some years before, that the EFTA states are liable under EEA law for damage and loss due to their breach of obligations under the agreement (see EFTA Court of Justice, 1998). This case was an instance of incorrect implementation of a directive. The court derived a state obligation from the stated purposes and legal structure of the EEA Agreement: namely, that a proper functioning of the EEA Agreement is dependent on individuals and economic operators being able to rely on those rights intended for their benefit. The court found that the objectives of homogeneity and establishing the right of individuals and economic operators to equal treatment and equal opportunities are so strongly expressed in the EEA Agreement that the EFTA states are obliged to provide for compensation for loss and damage caused to an individual by incorrect implementation of a directive.

In the *Finanger II* case, the Supreme Court accepted state liability as part of EEA law as implemented into Norwegian law (Norwegian Supreme Court, 2005). The court stated that it found the arguments of the EFTA Court convincing, and that liability for breach of the agreement must be viewed as a premise underlying the contracting parties' conclusion of the agreement. As such, it must also be regarded as having been included in the Norwegian Act that implemented the agreement into Norwegian law. At the same time, the court rejected a claim that there is a rule of liability under *Norwegian* law for breach of EEA obligations. This means that the EEA rule of liability forms the outer limits of liability of the state.

Judicial sovereignty

The setup of courts

The case law of the CJEU is an important part of the EU *acquis* – the agreement has a special provision in Article 6, ensuring its inclusion. The wording of this article is:

> Without prejudice to future developments of case-law, the provisions of this Agreement, in so far as they are identical in substance to corresponding rules of the Treaty establishing the European Economic Community and the Treaty establishing the European Coal and Steel Community and to acts adopted in application of these two Treaties, shall, in their implementation and application, be interpreted in conformity with the relevant rulings of the Court of Justice of the European Communities given

prior to the date of signature of this Agreement. (Official
Journal of the European Communities, 1994b)

As pointed out by the Court of Justice, this article, in its
wording, is limited to case law interpreting 'provisions' of the
agreement, and does not include the case law of the court as
a whole (see Opinion 1/91: Official Journal of the European
Communities, 1991, paragraph 27). It therefore excludes
important characteristics of EU law, such as supremacy and
direct effect.

The institutional judicial setup in the EEA is more complex
than in the EU. Article 108 specifies that the EFTA states shall
establish a court of justice. The EFTA Court is, however, not
an 'EEA Court' in the sense that the CJEU is the main court
of the EU. In Article 106, there is an arrangement to 'ensure as
uniform an interpretation as possible of the agreement' (Official
Journal of the European Communities, 1994b). The EEA
Joint Committee sets up a system of exchange of information
concerning judgments by the EFTA Court, the Court of
Justice of the European Communities and the Court of First
Instance of the European Communities and the Courts of Last
Instance of the EFTA states. This is done 'in full deference to
the independence of courts' (Official Journal of the European
Communities, 1994b). From this, we can draw the conclusion
that there are several 'EEA Courts' – each with an independent
and equal status. The reality, however, is somewhat different.

Together with Article 6 of the EEA Agreement, the
Surveillance and Court Agreement (SCA) creates a vertical
relationship between the CJEU and the EFTA Court, since the
EFTA Court is under an obligation to interpret the provisions
of the EEA Agreement in conformity with the relevant rulings
of the CJEU. In practice, however, the relationship is more of
a dialogue. The EFTA Court must often rule on issues where
there are no CJEU precedents. Here the EFTA Court takes
into account the case law of the CJEU, but cases decided by

the EFTA Court are also referred to by the Advocates General and the CJEU when similar issues arise in the EU. The two courts do not always agree. In the practical workings between the courts, homogeneity is understood as a process-oriented concept and it is not accurate to speak of lack of homogeneity when the two courts have differing views on a certain issue (Baudenbacher, 2015).

The relationship between the EFTA Court and the national courts in the EFTA states have at times been more strained, at least when it comes to Norway. In particular, two issues have given grounds for concern. The first is the reluctance of the Norwegian Supreme Court to refer cases to the EFTA Court, while the second is the status of the advisory opinion of the EFTA Court in the following national proceedings.

Referral of cases from national courts to EFTA Court

The relevant provision that governs the relations between national courts in the EFTA states and the EFTA Court is Article 34 SCA. This states in its first paragraph that 'the EFTA Court shall have jurisdiction to give advisory opinions on the interpretation of the EEA Agreement', and in the second paragraph that 'where such a question is raised before any court or tribunal in an EFTA State, that court or tribunal may, if it considers it necessary to enable it to give judgment, request the EFTA Court to give such an opinion'. In the third paragraph, it gives the EFTA states the possibility to determine that only courts of last instance shall have the right to request advisory opinions (Official Journal of the European Communities, 1994a).

There are clear parallels between the institution of advisory opinions from the EFTA Court and of preliminary rulings of the CJEU.[19] But there are also important differences. When compared with Article 267 TFEU, one main difference is that the CJEU gives 'preliminary rulings' whereas the EFTA Court gives advisory opinions. Another important difference is that the SCA does not include a duty for courts of last instance to refer cases to the EFTA Court. The CJEU emphasised such differences in its Opinion 1/91 where it considered the proposed arrangement that the EFTA states might authorise their courts to refer cases to the ECJ for its advisory opinion. The court rejected this by stating:

> In contrast, it is unacceptable that the answers which the Court of Justice gives to the courts and tribunals in the EFTA States are to be purely advisory and without any binding effects. Such a situation would change the nature of the function of the Court of Justice as it is conceived by the EEC Treaty, namely that of a court whose judgments are binding. Even in the very specific case of Article 228, the Opinion given by the Court of Justice has the binding effect stipulated in that article. (Official Journal of the European Communities, 1991, paragraph 61)

Through its case law the EFTA Court has developed what it has labelled *procedural homogeneity*. Procedural homogeneity entails that 'the EEA EFTA States should, by and large, live up to the same standards as the Union pillar with regard to the enforcement and effectiveness of rules, protection of rights, workings of the institutions, etc' (Magnusson, 2014). Based on this, some have argued that the EEA Agreement entails an obligation for national courts of last instance to refer cases to the EFTA Court. Although this has no basis in the wording of Article 34 SCA, such an obligation can be derived from the EEA Agreement itself – in particular, in its principle of loyalty in Article 3 and the general principle of access to justice and Recital 8 of the preamble to the agreement (Magnusson, 2014). The EFTA Court itself has stopped short of formulating a duty for the national courts in terms of 'obligation' but has used language that, in effect, implies the same. In its case in *Jonsson*, regarding social security for migrant workers, the court held that:

> It is important, in order to render the EEA Agreement effective, that ... such questions are referred to the Court under the procedure provided for in Article 34 of the Agreement between the EFTA States on the Establishment of a Surveillance Authority if the legal situation lacks clarity (Case E-18/11 Irish Bank, judgement of 28 September 2012, not yet reported, paragraphs 57 and 58). Thereby unnecessary mistakes in the interpretation and application of EEA law are avoided and the coherence and reciprocity in relation to rights of EEA citizens, including EFTA nationals, in the EU are ensured. (EFTA Court of Justice, 2013, paragraph 60)

It has been argued that not only the principles of loyalty, homogeneity and legal certainty entailed in the EEA Agreement, but also European Court of Human Rights (ECHR) Article 6's right to access to court demand that national courts of the EFTA states are under an obligation to refer matters to the advisory opinion of the EFTA Court. According to Magnusson, the role of the national judge in an EFTA state is, by and large, comparable to what would be the case in an EU state, and 'a great deal of responsibility for judicial protection under EEA law is placed on the national judiciary which, in turn, has to cooperate with the EFTA Court through the preliminary reference procedure when it is confronted with genuine and relevant questions of EEA law' (Magnusson, 2014, 131). Magnusson argues that the case law of the EFTA Court is a de facto recognised *acquis* of the EEA Agreement and, from this, together with the principle of loyalty, derives the national courts' obligation 'to make a referral to the EFTA Court and subsequently to comply with an advisory opinion when applying EEA law' (Magnusson, 2014, 131).

A main counterargument is that an important objective of having the EEA Agreement as an alternative to EU membership was to retain legislative and judicial sovereignty of the EFTA states (see also Fredriksen and Franklin, 2015). This sovereignty is undermined if the national courts of the EFTA states have an obligation to refer matters of EEA law to the EFTA Court. It was obviously an intention with the agreement that the 'judicial defence of these rights' referred to in Recital 8 of the preamble should and could be provided by the national courts of the EFTA states for matters arising under their jurisdiction (Official Journal of the European Communities, 1994b). The arrangement provided for in Article 106 EEA is clearly based on the perception of equality in status between the two European courts and the national courts of the EFTA states. This perception still informs the practice of the Supreme Court of Norway. The court does refer some cases, but more often makes a direct interpretation of EEA rules based on the jurisprudence of, above all, the CJEU. In its approach to the practice of the CJEU, the Supreme Court applies the provision in Article 3 (2) SCA.[20] This provision was formally only directed to the EFTA Court, but in applying it in its own practice, the Supreme Court clearly indicates its equal status to the EFTA Court in deciding difficult issues of interpretation regarding EEA and EU rules.

There may be many reasons for a national judge not to refer a case to the EFTA Court for an advisory opinion (see Bårdsen, 2013). National judges have pointed out some of these reasons. For one, the national court will often prefer to find a solution in national law if the EEA question is not specifically raised by any of the parties. For another, the parties often seem to prefer a solution by the national court, even if a question of EEA law is raised. To request an advisory opinion is cumbersome and demanding both for the parties and the court, and the parties are often not eager to stay the proceedings to wait for an opinion by the EFTA Court. In practice, referring cases to the EFTA Court usually prolongs the proceedings by a year or more.

The advisory nature of opinions from the EFTA Court

The EFTA Court has also insisted that the opinions it gives on EEA law are more than mere opinions. In its first cases, the court formally labelled the opinion it issued with 'Judgment of the Court' but the conclusion was introduced as 'the following Advisory Opinion' (EFTA Court, 1994). In an intermediate spell, the court labelled the opinions as 'Advisory Opinion' (EFTA Court of Justice, 1997). From 2000 onwards, the court went back to calling its opinions 'Judgment of the Court'.

The Norwegian Supreme Court in *STX* challenged the status of the opinions of the EFTA Court. This was a case regarding posting of workers and minimum rates of pay (Norwegian Supreme Court, 2013). The case concerned the interpretation of Directive 96/71/EC on the posting of workers, and whether the terms and conditions of employment in a collective agreement – which had been declared universally applicable and thus was mandatory within the industry concerned – was compatible with EEA law in the context of the posting of workers. The Norwegian Tariff Board had granted universal application to clauses contained within the agreement regarding the basic hourly wage, normal working hours, overtime supplements and a shift-working supplement, a 20% supplement for work assignments requiring overnight stays away from home and compensation for expenses in connection with work assignments requiring overnight stays away from home. The case was referred by the Borgarting Court of Appeals to the EFTA Court. The EFTA Court decided that directive 96/71/EC does not permit an EEA state to secure workers posted to its territory from another EEA state compensation for travel, board and lodging expenses when work assignments require overnight stays away from home, unless this can be justified based on public policy provisions.[21]

When the case reached the Supreme Court, this court unanimously found that compensation for travel, board and lodging expenses must be regarded as part of the minimum wages, according to the directive. In this, it explicitly came to the opposite interpretation to the EFTA Court. Regarding the status of the opinions of the EFTA Court in national courts, the Supreme Court said that it was not required to apply the opinion of the EFTA Court 'untested', but that it had a duty to form its own independent opinion with regard to the opinion of the EFTA Court. It followed from this that the Supreme Court was not formally prevented from applying a differing interpretation of EEA law.

The reactions to this from the EFTA Court were strong. In a speech at a conference in Norway, the president of the EFTA Court, Carl Baudenbacher, stated 'it ain't over until the fat lady sings' and proceeded to criticise the interpretation of EEA law that the Supreme Court had made in *STX*.[22] He then referred to the duty of the EFTA Surveillance Authority to enforce EEA law in cases where the national courts deviate from the opinion of the EFTA Court. He also argued for a duty of the Supreme Courts of the EFTA states to refer those cases to the EFTA Court where the EEA question is not obvious. In later statements he seems to accept the position that there is no obligation to refer cases to the EFTA Court, and that the referring court is not formally bound by the opinion. In a speech in London in October 2016 he said:

There is no written obligation from courts of last resort to make a reference and the preliminary rulings of the EFTA Court are not formally binding. I do not say that the Supreme Courts in the EFTA States are free to refer and free to follow or not. They are still bound by the duty of loyalty and the principle of reciprocity. But these are obligations that are difficult to enforce so, on balance, the EFTA States and their courts enjoy more flexibility. (Baudenbacher, 2016, 11)

On the other hand, the Supreme Court of Norway has consistently held that opinions and cases from the EFTA Court have a strong persuasive power. In cases where it has not asked the EFTA Court or not followed its case law, it has based its rulings on the case law of the CJEU (Fredriksen and Franklin, 2015, 674f). It is therefore inaccurate to say that the Norwegian court has developed its own national approach to EEA law.

Changes in the EU treaties

Within the EU, a major part of the development takes the form of treaty revisions. To mention some of the important ones: the Monetary Union, citizenship, closer cooperation in justice and home affairs and the Charter of Fundamental Rights. Such changes often have direct implications for the interpretation and application of the rules of the internal market. For instance, citizenship is of increasing importance to the development of the right to free movement of persons.

The EEA has no mechanism to formally update its rules after such changes in the EU. On the other hand, the EFTA Court interprets EEA law in light of new EU rules requiring this in order to maintain homogeneity between EEA and EU law, and the court 'is prepared to go to great lengths in order to maintain homogeneity between EU and EEA law' (Fredriksen and Franklin, 2015, 649). To the extent that the EEA rules are changed by interpretation, this means that legislation is changed without any collaboration from the EFTA countries. This can be a direct challenge to the sovereignty of the EFTA states, and can be illustrated by reference to the discussion on the effect of the Charter of Fundamental Rights in the EEA.

European Union law has seen expansive development regarding human rights and in its relationship to the ECHR since 1993 (for this development see Defeis, 2012). In 1992, the Treaty of Maastricht established the European Union and included in its Article F paragraph 2 a provision stating that

'The Union shall respect fundamental rights, as guaranteed by the European Convention for the Protection of Human Rights ... as general principles of Community law'. The Treaty of Maastricht was negotiated in parallel to the EEA Agreement, and is not reflected in the agreement. The commitment of the EU to the ECHR is now in a strengthened form in Article 6 TEU. The EU Charter was proclaimed in Nice in 2000. In the Treaty of Lisbon, the accession of the EU to the ECHR was required, and the charter was made part of the treaty. How, if at all, is this development reflected in the EEA?

The answer to this question varies depending on who one asks. The contracting parties have expressed different opinions (for an overview, see Wahl, 2014). The government of Norway argued in *ESA v Iceland* that the charter lacks direct relevance for the interpretation of the EEA Agreement because it has not been incorporated into it (EFTA Court of Justice, 2011, paragraph 163). Iceland, on the other hand, relied on the charter in the same case.

In a consistent line of cases, the EFTA Court has held that EU fundamental rights also form part of EEA law and fall under the jurisdiction of the EFTA Court (for an overview of cases, see Björgvinsson, 2015, 273ff). President Baudenbacher earlier declared that the EFTA Court has 'followed suit' with the CJEU in its longstanding tradition of referring to the ECHR and the case law of the European Court of Human Rights (Baudenbacher, 2005, 30). As pointed out by Fløistad (2004, 89), the question of the inclusion of human rights in the scope of the EEA Agreement is not one of being for or against human rights, but rather of whether the EFTA Court has been given the mandate to make the choices that balancing human rights against other rights and interests entail.

Legal doctrine is more reserved. Writing on the EEA and the ECHR, Björgvinsson points out that, from a formal point of view, the Convention does not form a part of the EEA Agreement as a binding source of legal norms in the context of the EEA Agreement. Still, the case law of the EFTA Court strongly supports the conclusion that the norms contained in the Convention – which also reflect a common standard and a common denominator for a minimum standard for the protection of fundamental rights on a European level – are a part of the general unwritten principles of EEA law (Björgvinsson, 2014, 276).

Fredriksen argues that fundamental rights and the EU Charter not only impose obligations on the states, but also on individuals. The question of the charter's relevance to the EEA must be assessed on a case-by-case basis, and homogeneity must yield to legal certainty when drawing upon EU law that is not formally part of the EEA Agreement will lead to the imposing of new obligations on private subjects or encroachments on the sovereignty of the EFTA states (Fredriksen, 2013, 378). Wahl, also writing on the status of the charter in the EEA, observes that it cannot be binding in the EEA context, but that, on the other hand, it cannot be outright excluded when interpreting and applying EEA provisions (Wahl, 2014, 295).

This development shows that perhaps the most challenging part of the relations between the EU and the EFTA states regarding sovereignty is the development of the EU that takes place outside of the EEA Agreement. The EU is a community in motion, and a third party that wishes to be tightly integrated with the EU must accept this.

Concluding reflections

Formally the EEA ensures upholding the sovereignty of the EFTA states and at the same time their participation in a dynamic legal community. This has only been possible through strong political commitments to sustain the EEA, and through a depoliticisation of the issues of legal reform. The main bulk of legal acts are of a purely technical nature and do not require a decision of the parliament. Nevertheless, a considerable amount of legislation is of more substance and political importance. This has not prevented the EFTA states from taking on board all new legislation of relevance that has been adopted by the EU. Between 1992 and 2011 there were only 17 cases where the issue of not accepting a new legal act was raised in the Norwegian parliament, notwithstanding the fact that the parliament was invited to take decisions on the inclusion of new legal acts in the agreement on 249 occasions (NOU 2012:2, 100, 103). This shows the low level of political debate in Norway over the adoption of new EU rules into the agreement.

The low level of conflict may reflect genuine lack of disagreement or it may be that disagreement is somehow kept away from affecting the process of decision making. We will address that in the next chapter. Another issue that requires attention when it comes to broader implications is the cumulative effects of norm and rule incorporation over time.

Since 2011 there has been an increasing backlog in the adaptation of new EU rules in the agreement and in the adoption of these rules in the internal legal orders of the EFTA states. There are several reasons for this backlog. One is that the question of EEA relevance of EU rules has become more complicated by the changes in EU competences through new treaties. The EEA Agreement is built upon the pre-Maastricht pillar structure of the EU, which is becoming obsolete, in particular through the restructuring of competences in the Lisbon Treaty. This means that new legal acts are often grounded in other policy areas in addition to the single market. An issue where questions have been raised in the EEA Committee is on the topic of civil and criminal sanctions, which the EFTA states maintain fall outside the scope of the EEA. Another issue is union citizenship, where the EU exerted 'considerable pressure' on the EFTA states to take over the Citizen's Directive (2004/38) (Dystland et al, 2018, 811).

A further complication is the increasing practice to bestow EU agencies with decision-making powers. Examples of this are the European Chemicals Agency (ECHA) and The Agency for the Cooperation of Energy Regulators (ACER). ACER was created by the Third Energy Package to further progress the completion of the internal energy market both for electricity and natural gas. Adoption of this regulatory package has been one of the most controversial issues in Norway under the EEA Agreement because of the powers bestowed on ACER. Since the EFTA states are not members of these agencies, endowing the agencies with powers to take decisions that are binding on citizens in these states entails constitutional issues in Norway and Iceland in particular. This complicates the internal processes in these countries, and contributes to the increasing time lag. In Norway it has also contributed to increasing the level of controversy over the EEA Agreement, both in political and in legal academic circles.

5

What can Britain learn from Norway's experience?

Brexit is about dealing with the trilemma of state sovereign control, democratic self-government and market access. The different circumstances surrounding Norway and the UK will not simply revolve around differences in bargaining strength, but rather in terms of the relationship between the pressures for continued market access, the contingent and complex process of bargaining, and the legal and normative principles and values involved, including political grandstanding/symbolic politics by all kinds of actors. The EFTA countries have ensured market access but at the expense of state sovereign control and democratic self-governing, not formally speaking, but in actual practice. In addition, these countries, as the Norway example testifies, have not confined the effects to market-related issues. Affiliation to the EU is therefore not simply a matter of market access but of incorporation in the broader legal and socioeconomic order that the EU has been constructing over time. The distinctive feature for the closely affiliated non-members is that the type of affiliation that they have chosen is akin to voluntary hegemonic submission (Eriksen and Fossum, 2015). The EU is not set up to be a hegemon but some of its relations to (non-)members are hegemonic in practice if not in their intents, because of the consistently articulated need to retain the integrity of the EU legal system, the *acquis*, when dealing with the association of non-members. In this, the political institutions of the EU are bound by the legal rationality of the CJEU. This has clearly and consistently been spelled out by the court since its Opinion 1/91 on the EEA Agreement. This will restrict also the type of association that the UK can obtain with the EU.

Squaring the circle for the UK

As we have seen in Chapter Four, the main challenge with regard to market access is sustaining equal rules and conditions over time, given the dynamic nature of the EU. The Norway model is dynamic so as to minimise the problems of market access. There is also the matter of compliance, which is closely monitored. There has been considerable expansion into related flanking areas, such as environmental and social affairs. In addition, the dynamic nature of Norway's association with the EU makes it difficult for Norway to prevent areas that have been explicitly excluded from the agreements being subsequently pulled into the EU's orbit. For Norway, a telling example is agriculture. It is politically very sensitive, and was explicitly excluded from the initial EEA Agreement. At present, 40% of the rules and regulations that Norway incorporates are in the field of agriculture as a result of the agreement on veterinary issues, presented above in Chapter Three. Important reasons for inclusion were the need for market access for fish and the sheer dynamics of spillover effects from related policy areas. These provisions are not confined to border-crossing activities but cover internal affairs: 'In practice today, this body of regulations makes up the main portion of all public regulation pertaining to production, sale, labelling, hygiene and so forth with regard to fish and agriculture in Norway and to a large extent sets the standards in both these sectors' (NOU 2012:2, 646-647; authors' translation). This is not simply a matter of trading off market access and state sovereign control. It shows how the affiliated non-member state loses control over an issue area that it explicitly sought to prevent being traded off against other issues. On the other hand, from the Norwegian point of view the main reason for excluding agriculture was to be able to maintain a system of subsidies that was deemed necessary to sustain thriving rural communities in a country where the conditions for large-scale farming are challenging. The reasons for excluding fisheries was to maintain national control with the management and exploitation of marine resources. These objectives, both in the agricultural sector and in fisheries, have been reached and maintained under the EEA Agreement, and Norwegian policies are not subject to EU control. A further problem that illustrates the dilemmas of trading off different considerations under circumstances of close and dynamic EU rule adoption is EU treaty change, as was discussed in Chapter Four.

In this chapter, we first show that the complex and composite Norway model yields a complicated tapestry of policies and means of enforcing homogeneity in the EU context. In the second section of the chapter, we provide a brief account of the distinctive politicisation–depoliticisation dynamic that marks the Norwegian political scene. That is one of the domestic reasons why Norway's broad and multifaceted panoply of associations with the EU has emerged. It is a story not of design but of adaptation, of recognising the need for a close affiliation and of trying to deal with a negative referendum decision that is very hard to square with a rapidly changing and dynamic world amidst profoundly asymmetric patterns of interdependence. In the final part of the chapter, we consider the democratic implications in more detail.

Norway's experiences

The issue of EU membership has been the most conflictual issue in Norway's post-war history, and it continues to animate people. This profoundly divisive issue has been politically contained and has not been allowed to shape Norway's dynamic EU adaptation, which proceeds almost without any friction (NOU 2012:2, 20). The EEA Agreement does not oblige the EFTA states to take on new EU legislation, but thus far in the 23 years of the EEA's existence Norway has never used its right to reject an update of the agreement. At the heart of Norway's relationship to the EU there is a paradox: there is very little political conflict surrounding the comprehensive, dynamic and extremely asymmetric process of adaptation whereas the EU membership issue is a deeply contested matter.

From a political perspective, it is important to consider how the circumstances surrounding matters of domestic control may often shift the emphasis from governing to conflict handling. The lack of external control and large-scale rule adoption feed into the domestic realm; this situation constrains and conditions the scope for exercising control, which often boils down to a matter of managing the domestic fallout from decisions made elsewhere (at EU level).

The Norwegian political system has depoliticised the dynamic process of EU adaptation. That has not been done through bypassing the political system, or the popularly elected bodies, for instance by establishing consociational arrangements or specific forums where elites can take decisions without direct popular input. All issues are, formally speaking, conducted through the parliament, the Storting. However, the Storting has been made toothless. Consider for example the Storting's European Consultative Committee. It relates to EU issues differently from what is the case in otherwise comparable Nordic EU member states (such as the very active Danish European Affairs Committee). An analysis of the Norwegian Committee's written transcripts revealed that there were very few debates; executives simply briefed the legislators on what was taking place; and the committee's work and deliberations were marked by a clear 'system-enforced consensus' and absence of debate on principled and constitutional issues (Fossum and Holst, 2014).

The political parties are deeply divided on the EU membership issue; and some parties – especially Det Norske Arbeiderpartiet (DNA) or Labour – are deeply divided internally as well. They seek to limit the political fallout by keeping the contentious EU membership issue off the agenda. At the same time, there are no attempts by parties to block the functioning of parliamentary democracy in other ways. There are no appeals to the populace to take unlawful action. All parties have served as opposition parties and have also had shorter or longer stints in power, or have supported governing parties during the period in which the EEA Agreement has been in place. In that sense we can say that all parties honour Norway's international obligations as formulated in the EEA Agreement and, when in opposition, they also honour the basic norm of serving as the 'loyal opposition'.

The political system has established a particular mechanism for handling EU matters, namely through *gag rules* (for this notion, see Holmes, 1995).[23] The gag rules are primarily expressed through government declarations or coalition agreements, which specify the government's commitment to maintain the present arrangement with the EU through the EEA Agreement. Each agreement posits that a political party that seeks to alter the status quo – actively seeking EU membership or revoking the EEA Agreement – will violate the coalition agreement. Especially for the large parties it is a Hobson's choice: if you seek to change the EU membership status quo you will be in breach of the coalition agreement and therefore unable to govern. Such agreements have been labelled 'suicide clauses' in the media (Fossum, 2010).

The so-called 'suicide clauses' sustain what is often referred to as a political compromise where the no-parties maintain Norway's status as a non-member, and the yes-parties are able to engage in binding European cooperation. Gag rules regulate the issue of formal EU membership; they do not regulate the ongoing and dynamic Norwegian incorporation in the EU. If anything, the gag rules have *simplified* the process of active adaptation, because the gag rules make it possible to decouple adaptation from the highly contentious issue of EU membership. The formal status of non-membership is politically important. It provides symbolic reassurance of constitutional-democratic sovereignty, and enables the no-parties to reassure their voters that as 'parties in the electorate' – those specific issues that the electorate associates that particular party with (see Muirhead, 2014) – they have successfully managed to keep Norway out of the EU.

The last five years or so have seen increased controversy over aspects of Norway's EU affiliation, but mainly on specific issues associated with specific EU directives. By taking attention away from the constitutional aspects of the affiliation the gag rules have kept the focus on single isolated issues. The gag rules help to detract attention from the *cumulative* effects of Norway's ongoing EU adaptation.[24]

In the following, we look more closely at the nature of this adaptation and situate it within a broader framework of modes of association. As part of that, we point to the specifics of Norway's mode of association. One such factor is a greater measure of predictability, which matters to the social legitimacy of Norway's EU relation. In that sense, the system of depoliticisation is complemented by a measure of norm- and rule-based predictability that less fixed modes of association do not deliver.

The multitude of models for associating with the EU

From the experience of Norway, we see that there is no 'clean model' for the association of a non-member state to the different policy areas of the EU. Norway has close cooperation with the EU covering almost all the policy areas of the EU, except for the customs union and foreign trade and the Monetary Union (euro). The way this cooperation is structured varies from the almost supranational relationship of the EEA to the forum for exchanging views and information on matters of common interest on defence policy. If we draw on the Swiss experience, we even see that the same policy areas can be accessed in ways that differ. We also see that separate ways of structuring the relationship have different consequences. The main point to take away from this is that there is not one template for the structuring of an agreement between the UK and the EU. The different models have elements that can be combined in many ways, and there is nothing that in principle prevents the parties from coming up with totally new elements. The use of an independent investment court system for dispute settlement in the EU-Canada Comprehensive Economic and Trade Agreement (CETA) is a further illustrative example (in addition to the other forms of dispute settlement that we have presented in this book) of this diversity.

The agreement presented in the Joint Report of the EU and UK negotiators on 8 December 2017 introduces yet other models of structuring sovereign control, democratic self-governing and market access. The agreement on citizen's rights locks conditions for acquiring the right of residence under the Withdrawal Agreement to Directive 2004/38/EC. There is no provision for a dynamic development in the rules to accommodate for new EU legislation. The matter of dynamic interpretation, however, is different. First of all, Article 35 states that the agreement should have direct effect, and that inconsistent or incompatible rules and provisions of national law shall be disapplied. The agreement also has provisions to ensure consistent interpretation of the rights of the citizens. It states in Article 38 that the CJEU is 'the ultimate arbiter of the interpretation of Union law', and that UK courts shall therefore have due regard to relevant decisions of the CJEU after the specified date (European Commission, 2017a). The agreement should also establish a mechanism enabling UK courts or tribunals to ask the CJEU questions of interpretation of those rights where they consider that a CJEU ruling on the question is necessary for the UK court or tribunal to be able to give judgment in a case before it. Consistent interpretation of the citizens' rights part should further be supported and facilitated by an exchange of case law between the courts and regular judicial dialogue.

The agreement on Ireland and Northern Ireland seeks to protect, 'in all its parts', the Good Friday or Belfast Agreement reached on 10 April 1998 by the UK government, the Irish government and the other participants in the multi-party negotiations. According to Article 49, the UK undertakes to 'maintain full alignment with those rules of the Internal Market and the Customs Union which, now or in the future, support North-South cooperation, the all-island economy and the protection of the 1998 Agreement' (European Commission, 2017a). The UK's intention is to achieve these objectives through the overall EU-UK relationship. The UK also undertakes to ensure that no new regulatory barriers develop between Northern Ireland and the rest of the United Kingdom. It is difficult to read this otherwise than that the UK undertakes not only to maintain in place the EU rules that it will adopt in the Withdrawal Bill, but also to dynamically introduce new EU legislation and to ensure application and interpretation consistent with the internal market of the EU. As we have seen, such 'dynamic homogeneity' is a precondition for 'full alignment with the rules of the Internal Market' and ensures that there are no regulatory barriers. The institutional solutions to ensure this have, however, not been addressed when it comes to the Irish question.

It is evident from the Norwegian model that association with the different policies is not necessarily an 'all or nothing' arrangement, notwithstanding this being the negotiation position of the EU. There are areas where this is the case, notably Schengen, and the Dublin cooperation on the state responsible for examining a request for asylum lodged in any of the participating states. Both these arrangements oblige the associated states to accept the whole body of the *acquis*, and to take on board all changes to this that are adopted by the EU. Failure to do this leads to the right for the EU to terminate the agreement. Both these agreements are in areas where national security concerns and state sovereignty traditionally are strong: the conditions for the admittance of third-country nationals into the territory of the state. Since people can move freely within the Schengen area, a deviation from the agreed criteria by one state will affect all the others. Within a comprehensive deal such as the EEA, this is different. Failure by the EFTA states to take on harmonised rules in one area, for example on the access to delivery of postal services, need not affect the provision of other services such as construction work or banking, or the other market freedoms. For this reason, the EEA Agreement Article 102 empowers the EEA Joint Committee to consider 'the part of an Annex to this Agreement which would be directly affected by the new legislation' (Official Journal of the European Communities, 1994b). The other parts of the agreement are from a strictly legal point of view unaffected by the refusal of the EFTA states to accept new EU legislation.

Even in a substantial sense there is no all or nothing. The Swiss agreements are an example of splitting up of the market freedoms. There is free movement of goods and persons. When it comes to services, there is no general arrangement, but there are agreements on some services, whereas most are not included. People have a right to provide services for a limited time as part of the free movement of persons. Legal bodies such as corporations and other business enterprises have no such right. Freedom of establishment extends to people, but not to legal bodies. Swiss corporations therefore may not freely establish branches in the EU or provide services without establishment, outside of the specific agreements. But Swiss nationals may seek work in the EU and vice versa. Switzerland also takes part in cooperation on research and development and programmes for exchange of students and academics.

The EEA is far from all-encompassing. Free movement of goods only includes goods originating in the EEA and is limited to goods specifically falling within the agreement and the protocols. This is a consequence of the fact that the EFTA countries are not part of the customs union or the foreign trade policy, and that agriculture and fisheries fall outside of the agreement. Lichtenstein has special arrangements on the free movement of persons that gives them the right to regulate the permanent settlement of nationals from other states.

There is a range of models for settling disputes between Norway and the EU. We have the shadow institutions of the EEA where the EFTA Surveillance Authority (ESA) and the EFTA Court perform the same functions regarding the EFTA states as the Commission and the CJEU do regarding the member states. Individuals have access to national courts and the EEA Agreement obliges the EFTA states to ensure that EEA law is enforceable, with predominance over national rules. National courts are bound to the case law of the CJEU from before the signing of the agreement, and are strongly encouraged to follow the subsequent case law as relevant to the interpretation of common rules. Cases can be referred to the EFTA Court for preliminary advisory opinions. If the national courts of the EFTA states do not follow the interpretations of the EFTA Court or the CJEU, the ESA may initiate infringement procedures if the EFTA state fails to change its laws for the future. If the result of such a procedure is a ruling by the EFTA Court, this ruling is binding on the EFTA state. Differences in interpretation may be addressed by the EEA Joint Committee. Failure to reach agreement here may lead to a suspension of that part of the agreement that is directly affected by the discrepancy, according to the provisions of Article 102.

Schengen and Dublin have different dispute settlement mechanisms. Individuals have access to Norwegian courts. There is no Schengen court to guide these in their interpretation. There is an objective that the applications in the Norwegian courts and the CJEU are as uniform as possible, and the Schengen Mixed Committee shall keep the development of the case law 'under close review'. If substantial differences develop, and the Mixed Committee is unable to settle these differences, the agreement is terminated. Up to now there have been no cases on the interpretation of Schengen rules in the Norwegian Supreme Court so the problem has not arisen.

The Swiss agreements have yet other models for dispute settlement. These also state that the relevant case law of the CJEU prior to the signing of the agreement is binding or shall be 'taken account of'. Subsequent case law shall be communicated to the Swiss. If differences in interpretation arise, each of the parties may bring the matter to the Joint Committee, which may settle the dispute. In the agreement on free movement of persons, there is no provision on termination or suspension of the agreement or parts of it if the parties do not reach an agreement. The agreement on air transport states that the Joint Committee may take 'appropriate measures'.

When it comes to substance, we see that having identical rules in association agreements with EU rules on the internal market does not necessarily lead to equal conditions of competition and equal treatment of individuals and economic operators. A main objective of the negotiators of the EEA Agreement was to overcome the obstacle of the Polydor ruling of the CJEU, where the court interpreted a provision in the free trade agreement with Portugal differently from the identically worded provision in the treaty of the European Economic Community. This objective was achieved, and the CJEU has confirmed that EEA rules are to be interpreted in the same way as the EU's own rules for the internal market (see the *Ospelt* case: Official Journal of the European Communities, 2003). The rules of a single market having the characteristics of a domestic market are inherently different from provisions of a free trade agreement, because a single market is an undertaking in shared law making, as an intrinsic part of European integration. This difference is paramount in the CJEU's approach to the Swiss agreements. The court here takes as its starting point that Switzerland did not join the internal market and did not subscribe to the project of an economically integrated entity with a single market. Swiss operators in the EU are therefore not protected against discrimination and may be treated as third-country operators compared to operators from within the EEA. Where the agreements do not specifically confer rights on Swiss subjects or operators in the market, they cannot expect treatment that is preferential to the treatment that any third-country operator receives. This is a main difference from the EEA, where operators from Norway, Iceland and Lichtenstein are accorded the same treatment as operators from within the EU itself.

The effects of not being treated according to the same standards as operators from member states of the EU are particularly noticeable in the field of services. The agreement on free movement of services gives persons the right to provide cross-border services for a period not exceeding 90 days, on the same terms as those imposed by that state on its own nationals (see Official Journal of the European Communities, 2002a, Annex I, Article 19, provided that the individual has the right or has been authorised in the home state. Annex III gives rules on the mutual recognition of professional qualifications (diplomas, certificates and other evidence of formal qualifications) (Official Journal of the European Communities, 2002a). Under the freedom to provide services directive of the EU, a member state may not make the provision of services from another member state subject to an obligation to obtain authorisation from or to make a declaration to their competent authorities if the service provider operates legally according to its home state rules. Freedom to provide services under a free trade agreement often goes no further than to accord the right to provide services under equal terms to domestic providers.[25] This means that where domestic providers of services are subject to requirements or authorisations, these requirements and authorisations may also be needed from foreign operators exercising their right to provide services. The member state where the service is provided may not impose an obligation on the provider from another member state to possess an identity document issued by its competent authorities specific to the exercise of a service activity, or enforce its requirements which affect the use of equipment and material which are an integral part of the service provided. This does not necessarily apply to providers of services under a free trade arrangement. It is not evident whether the CJEU will take the service directive or the free trade approach as a starting point when interpreting the service rules of the Swiss agreement.

In all this, we see that association with the EU and participation in the internal market can take many forms. At the core lies the acceptance of common rules and equal conditions for operators in the market. There also seems to be a trend that the more comprehensive the association, the greater the need for institutional arrangements to secure consistent application and interpretation. All arrangements, even the EEA, have political consultations and solutions as the last resort in case of disagreement between the parties. Such arrangements, however, lack the necessary certainty and efficiency to operate over broad fields or in areas where there is a special need for legal certainty and access to justice. To a certain extent this can be compensated for with 'cliff edges' and 'guillotine clauses', entailing that the cooperation is suspended if the parties do not reach agreement. There therefore seems to be a set of options determining the variety of models: loose and sector-based agreements with little in the way of institutional arrangements, in fields that to a lesser extent challenge regulatory powers in areas of social or economic importance; agreements in more important fields but with hard break-off clauses; and more comprehensive agreements, either with well-developed institutional arrangements such as the EEA, or with cliff-edges such as Schengen and Dublin. We see this in play in the agreement between the EU and the UK on the first phase of the negotiation. In the area of citizen's rights, where access to justice and legal certainty is an issue, there are institutional provisions on the operation of the courts. The agreement on Ireland and Northern Ireland does not address institutions, but based on the comprehensiveness of the declared intent it is reasonable to predict that institutions will be necessary both for updating the existing rules and for their interpretation and application.

The next section turns to the democratic implications of Norway's EU affiliation. The focus is on actual practice, from the perspective of citizens. It conveys that flexibility of arrangements does not easily translate to greater citizen influence and control.

Democratic implications: executive dominance and depoliticisation

It is well known that the EU is marked by executive dominance, but it is obvious, if not equally frequently asserted, that this feature would be even more pronounced in terms of Norway's EU association. The Norwegian parliament, the Storting, is unable to exert influence over decisions made in the EU; it acts as a glorified rubber-stamp. Executive–legislative relations in Norway are altered. If the Norwegian government wants any influence on EU decisions, it has to be proactive, thus limiting the scope for public consultation in Norway. Legislative acts are handled in the EEA system after the decision has been reached in the EU, and there is strong pressure to pass them rapidly and ensure legal homogeneity across the 31-member EEA. It follows that Norwegian civil society is one step behind the decision processes; it cannot act as a corrective to a process increasingly determined by external bodies.

In addition, the parties' handling of the EU issue through such mechanisms as gag rules are *exacerbating the democratic deficit*. They have been structured to permit issue-focused debate and contestation without this degenerating into political stalemate. Precisely because of this delinking, the citizens are not informed about the constitutional-democratic implications of what is going on. One aspect is the lack of alternative depictions of the core constitutional democratic developments in Europe and the issues that are at stake. Second is a tendency to focus on single issues, detracting attention from broader patterns and cumulative effects. Third is depoliticisation. The irony is that whereas the increasingly dense pattern of Norway's EU association brings issues together, the debates dislodge themselves from broader assessments by focusing on single issues.

In sum, we have seen that Norway's relationship to the EU is problematic from a constitutional-democratic perspective. We need more research if we are to understand the entire range of difficulties that this relationship engenders. We have shown how the consensus-seeking Norwegian political system deals with the highly controversial issue of EU membership and the ongoing EU adaptation process. Norway has devised its own way of handling the discrepancy between facts and norms that states bent on sustaining traditional notions of sovereign control experience in contemporary Europe. It is symptomatic in Norway that successive governments have not sought to adapt people's normative expectations a lot. There is a mix of pragmatism and disbelief, but very little political and public engagement with the rationales and the justifications that are otherwise drawn on in Europe for states pooling and sharing sovereignty.

Why is there so little opposition to this arrangement in Norway? One aspect is that the EU membership issue has been separated out from the issue of adaptation. But if the substance of adaptation is out of sync with Norwegian interests, we should still expect opposition and conflict. The reality is that there has been very little conflict.

The question is relevant because it is readily apparent that the cumulative effects of the rapid and dynamic EU adaptation undercut the main justification for non-membership: preserving sovereign control and democratic self-government. The fact that the EU membership issue has been singled out from the issue of EU adaptation has served to reduce conflict. A remarkable feature of Norway is the high level of trust in government (Olsen, 2017, 107), which has apparently *not* declined through EU adaptation. Why then the low level of conflict? We may briefly list four possible reasons. The first is that the changes are insignificant. That is implausible, especially when we think about the cumulative impact. The second and far more plausible explanation is that Norway as a small state is an adaptive non-member, with a history of rapid adaptation to the external world. But that does not tell us much about the high levels of trust. A third reason could be that Norway's EU relationship is one of 'virtual representation'. Norway is virtually represented in EU decisions in the sense that EU laws often correspond with its interests. That certainly applies in some key issue areas such as the environment. Perhaps more important in terms of trust is that the EU is not an affront to the Norwegian socioeconomic model. The fourth and perhaps most important reason is that Norway has developed a comprehensive system to *compensate* for negative effects of EU adaptation through a well-functioning state; a very comprehensive public welfare system and social security net; and a very substantial fiscal buffer (the large pension fund is a case in point).

Concluding reflections: how transferable are Norway's lessons to the UK?

Three issues crop up when discussing the transferability of Norway's experiences to the UK. One is the issue of direct transferability. We need to understand the main similarities and differences between the UK and Norway if we are to get a clear sense of the scope for transferability. The second is to think of transferability more broadly, in terms of broader diagnoses or patterns rather than specific lesson-transfers. The third is to consider what the Norway model signifies – it is a matter of, on the one hand, the particular relationship that Norway has with the EU and, on the other hand, with the domestic handling of this relationship.

One important lesson from the Norway case is the importance of the structure (proximity) of the relationship. Applied to the UK, the question is whether the UK's far greater power and international salience will enable it to negotiate a superior arrangement to that of Norway. The question is how much of its power can be transferred into the bargaining process, especially if the UK seeks to stake out an unprecedented arrangement with the EU that maximises both EU market access and national control. The problem for the UK is that the more it stresses independence from the EU, the greater the demands from business, nations (Scotland and Northern Ireland) and citizens (especially EU citizens and young people) for EU access and rule and norm predictability. Conversely, the more the UK seeks continued EU rule/norm alignment, the more vulnerable it is to criticism from Brexiteers for reneging on the promise to regain control and betraying the vote in favour of Brexit.

If the structure of the relationship (and not the specifics of formal agreements that states negotiate with the EU) matters most, then the issue is less about UK bargaining strength and more about what the EU does. If the EU is able to sustain a united front, and stick to the rules in place, the UK will face difficult choices. This is not only a political issue within the EU, but also a legal issue. The CJEU has power to restrict the room for political manoeuvre in the EU's dealings with third countries, a power it has used several times, such as when negotiating with the EFTA countries and when considering accession of the EU to the European Convention on Human Rights. The court also sets the conditions for accepting outsiders into the internal market, as we have seen in its case law on Switzerland.

Difficulties mount up if tensions arise inside the UK, from opposition parties, or from devolved nations.[26] If the EU fails to sustain a united front and starts making concessions to the UK, these will percolate through the EU system and may generate internal dynamics in the EU that the UK can utilise to its advantage. Nevertheless, the main lesson we can derive from the manner in which states structure their associations with the EU is that the key determinant is the EU, not the UK.

A second lesson from Norway has been the dynamic nature of EU rule adaptation and the need for predictability. For the UK post-Brexit, and as noted above, EU rules and norms will be entrenched in the European Union Withdrawal Bill. The bill will repeal the European Communities Act of 1972 (ECA), which constitutes the legislative underpinning of the UK's EU membership. At that point, EU law in place in the UK becomes UK law. This is a legal structure which is similar to that of Norway within the EEA. In other words, the Withdrawal Bill sets up a structure that is highly conducive to ongoing norm adaptation. It ensures that EU law in the UK is no longer handled from the EU level, but from the UK level. This gives a very special twist to the notion of 'taking back control', because it underlines the need to consider issues of control not merely in the light of bargaining processes and outcomes but in terms of the dynamics of norm and rule adaptation. Reasserting control for the UK then means going through this enormous volume of regulations and directives, and determining which ones should be altered, and which ones should be kept.

Rule adaptation is for Norway a constant through the dynamic nature of the EEA and the Schengen agreements; for the UK it takes on a new shape after Brexit. In any case, both the UK and Norway face rule adaptation as a fact and as intrinsically related to the large body of EU law that they have already incorporated and that informs the operations of their political and administrative systems. The question is what difference it will make that the UK incorporates EU law directly into its domestic system at the very same time that it gives up its share of control over the making of EU laws. One difference from Norway's situation is that without an institutional provision to address it, there will not be a setup where the EU and the UK routinely agree on changes that the UK undertakes to make in its legislation to reflect changes in EU law. Another difference may stem from how the UK changes the role and status of incorporated EU rules through the Withdrawal Bill. The Europeanised element of UK law will get increasingly out of sync with EU rules and norms, heightening uncertainty. The UK will still, as does Norway, face strong domestic pressures for retaining as much rule contiguity as possible. Since the single market is a seamless web, that pressure will work across issues. The UK will have to deal with the conflicting pressures for EU norm conformity and domestic divergence as an 'insider' in relation to EU rules and norms, because it has been so extensively EU programmed.

A third lesson from Norway pertains to the manner in which the stress on internal sovereign control on the one hand reinforced the executive and on the other shifted to conflict management through depoliticising the EU adaptation process. In Norway, the deeply politicised issue of EU membership, a core constitutional issue, was contained and not permitted to intervene in the rapid and dynamic process of EU adaptation. In the UK, an almost opposite politicisation logic has unfolded: single issues, such as the metric standard (Morgan, 2005) or bent cucumbers, have been raised to fundamental issues of loss of control and sovereignty and have been linked to the

EU membership issue. The very different politicisation–depoliticisation dynamics in Norway versus the UK are bound to show up in the UK's EU relationship. It appears very unlikely that the UK political system is going to be able to curtail or contain political conflicts in the way Norway has done.

Brexit is pushed ahead by the fact that the EU membership issue has been politicised *for so long* (Lord, 2015) and, further, that it is quite easy to link single issues to the EU membership question. The UK political system is politicisation-prone: the political style is quite confrontational, intensified by a first-past-the-post electoral system that usually allows the largest party to take all power with the result that the costs of losing are unusually high; and a highly confrontational tabloid press (perhaps in particular on EU matters). In contrast, the Norwegian political system is marked by a very high trust in government; a strong consensus-seeking political culture; a proportional electoral system that never produces single-party majority governments; and a far more facts-oriented media scene. The UK is therefore unlikely to achieve a similarly depoliticised relationship with the EU, which means overall a less predictable relationship.

A fourth lesson from Norway is the strong element of executive dominance. There are many indications to the effect that the Brexit process will be an executive-led process. Concerns are raised that executive dominance will mark the process of altering the body of law that the Withdrawal Bill will include (Fowles, 2017). This body of law has significant relevance for the devolved nations, which are concerned about the loss of devolved powers and the principle of subsidiarity. The manner in which the Withdrawal Bill process is conducted will be of great importance for the future functioning of UK parliamentary democracy.

Fifth, both Norway and the UK exhibit a strong gap between facts and norms in the realm of sovereign control. We saw that there are different politicisation dynamics in the UK, which are likely to affect the relationship between substantive and symbolic politics. In Norway, the strong membership opposition was kept separate from and did not affect policy substance (read rapid and dynamic EU adaptation in a broad range of policy fields). In the UK the government will probably face a far more difficult task of trying to bridge the gap between the reality of interdependence and the strong normative attachment to sovereign control. In Norway politicians were able to manage this without addressing the EU's justifications; that seems difficult for the UK.

Finally, the UK is adaptive. Its far greater size suggests that it does not need to be as adaptive as a small state such as Norway. However, the UK is very unlikely to emulate Norway on the degree of trust in government or in terms of the broad compensatory socioeconomic arrangements that Norway has to buffer against various types of negative effects.

This brief assessment suggests that the different circumstances surrounding Norway and the UK will not simply revolve around differences in bargaining strength, but rather in terms of how the UK works out the relationship between the pressures for continued rule and norm adaptation; how it manages the contingent and complex process of bargaining; and how it relates to the normative principles and values involved, including political grandstanding/symbolic politics by all kinds of actors.

6

Would Britain be an 'elephant in the boat'?

It is widely acknowledged that Brexit will have significant effects for Norway.[27] Norway is by far the biggest state in the EEA, but if the UK, with its far greater population, power and international bargaining clout, joins the EEA, it will surely be the 'elephant in the boat'. Whether the elephant is good-tempered or bad-tempered matters, but regardless of the mood, its presence will be felt.

As this book has shown, the Brexit process is far too unwieldly and unpredictable to provide us with a clear indication of its eventual outcome. The range of possible outcomes remains very wide – from Brexit without any agreement to continued UK import of EU norms and rules (whether as a member or not). It is therefore necessary to operate with a number of different Brexit scenarios when trying to assess effects on associated non-members such as Norway.

In principle, since non-members have not pooled or shared sovereignty in the EU, one might assume that a closely associated non-member such as Norway would have more leverage in sorting out its future relationship with the UK than would

EU member states. However, several factors limit the scope of action for Norway. The Norwegian government has repeatedly underlined that it should not be treated as a third party because it is so closely affiliated with the EU. Nevertheless, because it is only an affiliated *non*-member it is not present in the negotiations between the UK and the EU (it lacks a seat in the European Council that issues the EU's negotiation guidelines; it has no political representation in the Council formations; and no representatives in the European Parliament). Nor will Norway be able to reach a bilateral settlement with the UK until there is an agreement between the EU and the UK, due to the exclusive competence in the common commercial policy, the UK cannot sign trade agreements with third parties until it has formally exited the EU.[28] Norway therefore has very limited influence on the terms of the UK's exit. That of course also extends to the terms of the UK's future association with the EU, which will also determine the UK's relationship with the EEA.

The Brexit process generates a new type of triangular relationship among Norway, the UK and the EU, where Norway is a mere receiver of the terms, as these are worked out and settled by the EU and the UK. That also means that Norway's terms of negotiations with the UK will to a large extent be determined by the negotiations between the UK and the EU, and whatever set of agreements they come up with. In the short run, there is hardly any scope for Norwegian influence; in the long run, and once the terms of the EU–UK relationship are established, there may be some wiggle-room for Norway, but again subject to the constraints built into the EU–UK agreements (insofar as they ensue).

In the following, we first provide a brief overview of the Norwegian government's objectives in relation to the EU and the UK. Thereafter, we discuss the possible effects on Norway with reference to a range of different EU–UK–Norway scenarios.

What are the objectives of the Norwegian government?

When discussing the Norwegian government's objectives, we need to focus on the form of association that the Norwegian government prefers, and to what extent that view is likely to materialise. That includes establishing whether there might be actors that could alter or block it within the Norwegian political establishment, among economic stakeholders or among citizens.

There is no question that prior to the Brexit referendum, the Norwegian government wanted the UK to remain in the EU. That view was quite widely shared across Norwegian society. There were some in Norway that associate Brexit with new political opportunities, but they are in the minority. After the Brexit referendum, the Norwegian government's ministers for EEA and EU affairs (Frank Bakke Jensen was replaced by Marit Berger Røsland on 20 October 2017 and her position was removed as part of a government reshuffle in January 2018) have repeatedly stressed that the government wants to maintain the EEA Agreement and Norway's other agreements with the EU. In addition, they underline that it is important that there is an orderly Brexit, and the government wants its post-Brexit relationship with the UK to be as close as possible. This applies equally to the short and the long term: the period of transition as well as the future long-term relationship. At the same time, the government is concerned that the solutions that are negotiated between the UK and the EU will ensure a well-functioning market within the *entire EEA* – that is, for the EEA members as well as for the EU members. Since Norway is not present at the negotiations, and since the Withdrawal Agreement will not include the EEA countries, this is an important concern for the Norwegian government.

Whether governments abide by their formal declarations hinges on a number of factors. One is the question of basic interest; another is the underlying constellation of power and dependence. With these considerations in mind, which relationship will the Norwegian government prioritise among the ones that Brexit has put in play: internal-EEA; the relationship to the EU; or the relationship to the UK (and the various parts of which it is made up)?

The EU is by far Norway's most important trading partner and associate in most fields. This is not only a matter of trade and economic (inter)dependence; it is about geographical location, historical bonds and other forms of institutionalised relations. After all, the EU subsumes under it Norway's close Nordic associates, Denmark, Sweden and Finland, which means that the context of Nordic cooperation has become very strongly Europeanised. Norway's Nordic association has had direct effect on its priorities and decisions in relation to the EU. A case in point is when Denmark, Finland and Sweden entered the Schengen agreement. Then, Norway had to ask for a Schengen association agreement in order to preserve the Nordic Passport Union. Had it not done so, the 1650 kilometre-long border between Norway and Sweden would have become the EU's external border, with Norwegians facing border controls when wanting to enter Sweden. That would have represented a dramatic change, since this border has been open for more than two centuries.

Norway has many interests in common with the EU's Nordic and continental member states. It is a strong defender of a social market economy and supports a significant role for the public sector in shaping society. It is well known for its progressive policies on gender equality and sustainable development. And even if the present Norwegian government underlines the central role of transatlantic relations and NATO in Norway's foreign and security policy (Meld.St.36, 2016-2017), it remains a fact that successive Norwegian governments 'have sought to establish as close an affiliation as possible with the EU's foreign and security policy' (Sjursen, 2015, 204-5).

Norway also has strong historical and contemporary bonds with the UK, from trade to defence. The two states share a restricted vision of the EU's political development in the sense that neither wants the EU to become a full-fledged federal state. Further, the UK is Norway's largest single state market for goods (including oil and gas, with Norway providing one-third of the UK's annual consumption of natural gas) and services. That amounts to well over NOK 200 billion per year (Røsland, 2017a). A critical component is of course made up of exports of oil and gas. The Norwegian government assumes that oil and gas exports will continue unaffected by Brexit (Bakke-Jensen, 2017a). As an EEA member Norway has signed up to free movement across the entire pre-Brexit 31-member EEA area, as noted above. There are around 20,000 Norwegian citizens in the UK and around 14,500 UK citizens in Norway, all of whom will be directly affected by Brexit (Røsland, 2017b). The Norwegian government has sought and obtained assurances from Prime Minister May that the terms offered to EU citizens in the UK will also be extended to Norwegian and other EFTA country citizens.[29] The EU has responded positively to this. However, the terms need to be worked out, because Norway, as noted, is not included in the agreement 'in principle' that was signed on Friday 8 December 2017 (European Commission, 2017a).

The general impression is that the Norwegian government's strong commitment to the need to retain the EEA Agreement is in line with the basic configuration of Norwegian interests and historical and contemporary bonds. At the same time, the bonds to the UK are very strong; if a conflict were to ensue between the EU and the UK there would be hard choices. At present there is strong support across Norway's political establishment and society for Norway's current EU arrangements; no veto actors that may topple this are apparent. However, whether that will continue to be the case hinges on how Norway handles the process and even more so on how the process unfolds.

How does the Norwegian government handle the Brexit process?

As has been pointed out in the above, the Norwegian government sits in the waiting room when it comes to the negotiations between the EU and the UK. This is not only an awkward position to be in regarding the international context, it is also awkward in relation to domestic society. It brings up a possible distinction between what we may term governmental preparedness as opposed to societal preparedness. How the government understands the situation and what it sees as opportunities and constraints may be out of sync with how the population understands these. In Norway's case that is a likely scenario given the long tradition of depoliticising EU issues, and the fact that the Norwegian political apparatus is hard-wired to treat EU issues as international rather than domestic. A knowledge and information gap may give rise to legitimacy problems, particularly if there are significant or dramatic changes afoot. These are considerations that we need to keep in mind when we consider in more detail how the Norwegian government is handling the Brexit process.

When the referendum result was known, Norway was no exception to the international norm: there was no plan B in case the UK voted in favour of leaving the EU. The Norwegian government has established an internal cross-ministerial working group to go through the existing agreements,[30] in order to establish what kinds of agreements will be needed in the various sectors of the economy in order to retain as close a relationship as possible after the UK leaves the EU and the EEA. The Ministry of Foreign Affairs and the Ministry of Trade, Industry, and Fisheries have established a reference group with domestic stakeholders[31] in order to get a clear sense of how the various interests are affected, and how they should best be defended. The Norwegian government seeks to be kept up-to-date on the negotiations from both the EU and the UK sides of the triangular relationship. The European Commission's Brexit negotiator Michel Barnier has met with and updated Norwegian diplomats after each round of Brexit negotiations. There are meetings within the EEA structure combined with frequent meetings at ministerial and administrative levels with EU and UK officials.[32] Norwegian Prime Minister Erna Solberg and other central Conservative party officials have also attended Brexit briefings under the auspices of the EPP in the European Parliament (Dagens Næringsliv, 2017). The government has recently withdrawn its plea for the chairmanship of the Organisation of Security and Cooperation (OSCE) in Europe, citing the added workload associated with Brexit as one of the main reasons for this.

There have been criticisms from those that say the Norwegian government is sitting on the fence; and these critics have been urging the government to start negotiations with the UK as soon as possible.[33] Part of that relates to concerns as to how high up on the list of the UK's priorities Norway will be. After all, the UK has pledged to sign agreements with large parts of the world, and has a very broad range of issues that it needs to sort out in order to ensure its future trade, financial and other concerns (Hansen, 2017).

As was pointed out in Chapter One, the UK is a pluri-national state with the various parts diverging on what kind of Brexit they seek. If we look at the statements by Norwegian government ministers, the general impression is that when they are discussing Brexit and the relationship between Norway and the UK, they generally refer to the UK *in singular terms*; there is no specific singling out of Scotland or any other UK nation. There is of course awareness in Norway of, for instance, Scotland's affinity for Norway and its preference for the EEA Agreement, but there are no official Norwegian efforts to prioritise this particular relationship.

The general impression we get from the manner in which the government handles the Brexit process is that this is organised as an executive-run process, combined with an element of stakeholder democracy, with parallels to the long Norwegian tradition of societal corporatism. The main dividing line in terms of preparedness therefore does not run between government and society, but between insiders in government and those in organised interest groups that the government consults on the one hand, and citizens or general civil society, which figures mainly as outsiders, on the other. It remains a low-key and quite depoliticised process. It is therefore difficult to know beyond government assurances how well prepared Norway is to face up to the challenges that the volatile Brexit process throws up. There is little information to be gained from the other side of the North Sea. The general impression is that the UK's Brexit debate is UK-centred. There is no discussion of the possible effects of Brexit on closely associated EU non-members such as Norway.

Four possible scenarios

In the following, we discuss the possible effects of Brexit on Norway with reference to four different scenarios. The focus is on two main dimensions. One dimension refers to the possible effects of the future nature of the EU–UK association; the other refers to the possible effects of the EU's development and how that may structure the triangular EU-UK-Norway relations. The EU has in the aftermath of the poly-crises launched a process of reform to deal with the fallouts of the many crises, and to prepare itself for the post-Brexit period.

Scenario 1: No EU–UK association agreement

This is the scenario that most actors seek to avoid. As noted in Chapter One, Prime Minister May said earlier that no deal is better than a bad deal. In discussing this scenario, we have to consider two possible trajectories. One is that there is no agreement at the point of formal UK exit, in other words, on 30 March 2019. That is unlikely given the recent agreement on the first phase of negotiations under Article 50 (although this still has to be signed off within a treaty framework). But at this point it cannot be entirely ruled out. There is still a possibility of blowback from a breakdown in the difficult stage two negotiations on the UK's future agreement with the EU that are unfolding as this book is going to press.

The other possible trajectory is that no agreement ensues after a period of transition. The assumption at present is that there will be a two-year period of transition to prepare for Brexit.[34] It is entirely conceivable that negotiations will terminate during this period, in which case there is no deal and the actors will face a cliff-edge at the end of that period. Or it may be that at the end of the transition period some issue areas will be agreed, whereas negotiations will stretch out much longer in other issue areas. The gravity of effects then hinges on which issue areas are agreed and which are not. This in turn will depend on the UK's insistence on bespoke agreements across the board.

The time factor and the complexity of the issues at stake yield a range of possible no-deal options. The critical issue is not whether there is a deal at a given point in time but whether there is a breakdown in trust between the key actors involved. That is the most problematic scenario, because as long as there is trust, actors are likely to be willing to offer extensions. The EU is under a treaty-based obligation to negotiate in good faith,[35] but is not under an obligation to reach an agreement.

If no agreement is struck and actors are not willing to continue negotiations, then within the area of trade the UK would revert to WTO rules. That would entail tariffs, the termination of mutual recognition frameworks and numerous other obstacles, including customs checks (Eeckhout and Patel, 2017). The question is what it would entail, more precisely. The WTO's Director-General Azevêdo has said that '[the UK] will be a member with no country-specific commitments' (Elliott, 2016).

The UK has been a member of the WTO through being an EU member; at Brexit it would have to negotiate the specifics of its WTO membership, which would take time. Others argue that the UK retains its rights and obligations. These are incomplete and need to be dealt with, but some hold that it may not be overly difficult (Bartels, 2016).

Breakdown through lack of trust will most likely have repercussions far beyond the failure to strike a trade deal, and may include such areas as security and defence, policing, civil justice cooperation, and research and development. The stakes are very high.

For the EU's non-members, failure to strike a trade deal would mean that they would face the prospect of tariffs at the moment of Brexit, a fear that the Norwegian Business Association (NHO) has voiced at several instances. The non-members will have to negotiate their terms of trade and access with the UK, most likely on a bilateral basis. The effects will depend on the extent to which the UK would set in motion a race to the bottom in social and environmental terms. It has recently been argued that, for instance in the area of gender relations in the UK, in particular under Conservative governments, the EU has been the main instigator of regulations pertaining to maternity rights (Guerrina and Masselot, 2018), and in particular a hard Brexit would jeopardise these with possible spillover beyond the UK. A hard Brexit would of course reintroduce uncertainty pertaining to the rights of citizens in the UK and in the non-member states. Even though these seem to be ensured by the joint commitments expressed by the parties on 7 December, the commitments are made under the caveat that 'nothing is agreed until everything is agreed'. There are other pressing areas such as developing a proper system for fisheries management because the UK will have large stretches of ocean, and fisheries management is a very important issue for Norway. Norway exports large quantities of fish to the UK; issues of hygiene and veterinary rules arise when the UK is no longer included in the same set of rules and regulations; and the question of quotas and access to fishing resources re-emerges. At present, the UK holds a large share of the EU's fishing quotas (Hansen, 2017). The point is that for Norway (and other affected fishing nations) there will be a need not only for ensuring market access, but for redesigning the entire regulatory regime.

Scenario 2: UK association agreement with the EU *outside* the context of the EEA

The UK government has consistently argued that none of the off-the-shelf alternatives that are available to it will work. At the same time, as the process has proceeded, it has become increasingly clear that '[i]t is unlikely that the EU would accept highly bespoke transitional arrangements, as this would be considered too complex and difficult to negotiate and implement in, and for, such a short period of time' (Eeckhout and Patel, 2017, 4). Despite UK Brexit Minister David Davis' intention of completing the agreement in October 2018, it is becoming increasingly likely that the transition period will not simply be one of implementation which Davis wants, but continued negotiations, given the range of issue areas, the complex nature of the issues involved, and the complex actor constellations that are involved. This scenario is therefore mainly relevant for the UK's *long-term* EU relationship; it will probably only become manifest well after the transition period is over.

The EU is not willing to grant a Swiss-type option to the UK, and in any case, if the direction of the present EU–Swiss negotiations is anything to go by – Piris (2017) refers to a leaked document – the UK is unlikely to find this acceptable. The Turkey model is highly unsatisfactory for the UK. Brexit Minister Davis has recently said that the UK will want to opt for a trade agreement that resembles the Comprehensive Economic and Trade Agreement (CETA) that the EU recently negotiated with Canada, but an extended version of it. The CETA agreement removes customs barriers for trade but only includes some services, and is inadequate in strategic areas for the UK such as banking and finance, pharmaceutics, auto production and aviation.[36] On the other hand, since it does not cover free flow of workers, it would enable the UK to regulate migration.

For the EU's non-members the main effect would be long and protracted EU-UK negotiations, and the uncertainty associated with those. A set of bespoke agreements would bring up questions not only of access to the UK market but the terms under which such access would be available for EU non-members, and no less importantly *when* these terms are to be settled. Some Norwegian commentators see opportunities, for instance in terms of gaining improved access for Norwegian processed fish, which could mean restoring parts of the Norwegian processing industry that moved out of Norway as a consequence of the EEA Agreement. At the same time, this scenario also brings with it the prospect of politicising Norway's EU relationship, especially insofar as the UK obtains a set of agreements that can be seen as superior to those that Norway has (Hansen, 2017). That could put the EEA Agreement in play. The other EEA countries could also set such processes in motion.

Scenario 3: UK association agreement with the EU *within* the context of the EEA

This is the most likely scenario for the transition period, as is also apparent from statements by EU and UK officials. There are several transition options that could be roughly speaking grouped under this scenario. Out of the five transition arrangements that Eeckhout and Patel (2017) mention, the following place the UK within the EEA: (a) extension of the EU *acquis communautaire*, without membership; (b) extension of the Article 50 withdrawal negotiations; and (c) remaining in the internal market via the EEA Agreement. The fourth option, that of remaining in the internal market by negotiating a new agreement modelled on the EEA Agreement, would locate the UK inside EFTA. It is only the last and least likely option, that of entering into a customs union agreement with the EU customs union, that is not broadly speaking relevant to the EEA. The two first options would basically preserve the present institutional structure, with the UK mimicking Norway's situation of being a rule follower, whereas options three and four would entail that the UK would be somehow included in or associated with the EEA institutional structure.

The main point here is that in all the most realistic transition scenarios some aspects of the Norway model figure prominently. For Norway, the two first options represent the least degree of disruption, because it would not activate the need for managing the complex trilateral relationship until the transition period is over.

Nevertheless, there are important legal considerations built into the choice of options that pertain to the transition period and to the period after. If the parties opt for the extension of the *aquis*, the question of surveillance and judicial functions arises. It may be that the UK agrees to submit to the surveillance of the Commission and the jurisdiction of the CJEU for a transition period, modelled on the arrangement agreed in the 7 December report. Another alternative could be to borrow the institutions of the EEA and EFTA, either by incorporating the UK into the EEA Agreement as a full contracting party or by other arrangements (options three and four above).

The UK is already a party to the EEA Agreement. According to Article 127, 'each Contracting Party may withdraw from this Agreement provided it gives at least twelve months' notice in writing to the other Contracting Parties' (Official Journal of the European Communities, 1994b). It has been maintained that notwithstanding this provision, withdrawal of a member state from the EU entails automatic withdrawal from the EEA, as the EEA is comprised of the EU with its member states, and the EFTA states, Norway Iceland and Lichtenstein.[37] Practically, the question of withdrawal is of little relevance, since the agreement ceases to apply to the territory of the UK once it withdraws from the EU (Arnesen 2018, 947). This follows from the provision in Article 126 (1) which states that 'the Agreement shall apply to the territories to which the Treaty establishing the European Economic Community (20) is applied' (Official Journal of the European Communities, 1994b).

Formally, however, a withdrawal is necessary. This follows from Article 127. Article 2, which provides the definition of 'contracting party'. This provision states that:

> the term 'Contracting Parties' means, concerning the Community and the EC Member States, the Community and the EC Member States, or the Community, or the EC Member States. The meaning to be attributed to this expression in each case is to be deduced from the relevant provisions of this Agreement and from the respective competences of the Community and the EC Member States as they follow from the Treaty establishing the European Economic Community.

The first question then is what can be 'deduced from' Article 127? Does 'contracting party' here refer to the Community and the EU member states, the Community, or the EU member states? The answer is not obvious. On the one hand, the whole point of the agreement is to tie the three EFTA states in with the internal market of the EU. On the other hand, the rights of these states and their citizens will be affected by agreements they have not been party to if a withdrawal agreement between the EU and one of its members would entail that operators in the EFTA states automatically lose their rights within the state that withdraws from the EU. This suggests that the procedure in Article 127 must be followed, and that there is no automatic withdrawal of the departing member state from the EEA. This does not mean that the state in question has a right to remain in the EEA, only that the withdrawal from the EEA must be done in an orderly fashion in accordance with the agreement (Hillion 2018, 959). The next question then is whether an exiting member state has the right to remain in the EEA by refusing to notify its withdrawal. Both substantive and formal arguments may be invoked against such a solution.

The substantive arguments are that the EEA Agreement is not designed for the participation of contracting parties that are not a member of either the EU or the EFTA (Hillion, 2018, 959). Such a party would not be subject to the jurisdiction of any of the courts or surveillance mechanisms that are central to the main characteristics of the EEA Agreement. The UK would therefore either have to negotiate an arrangement with the EFTA states to be subject to the jurisdiction of the EFTA Surveillance Authority and the EFTA Court, or with the EU to be subject to the jurisdiction of the Commission and the CJEU. For reasons of reciprocity, the other parties to the EEA Agreement would have to give their approval to such an arrangement within the EEA.

The formal arguments concern which party it is that must notify withdrawal from the EEA Agreement according to Article 127: the EU or the withdrawing member state. The wording suggests that this must be decided according to the division of competences in EU law. There seem to be persuasive arguments for the case that even though the EEA was concluded as a mixed agreement according to EC law at the time, the competence to act on the EEA Agreement according to Article 207 TFEU today lies with the Commission exclusively (Vedder, 2018, 118). This would suggest that the UK's right to withdraw from the EEA and negotiate in the proceeding diplomatic conference lies with the EU and not the UK.

The conclusion to this is that if the UK should wish to remain in the EEA after it has ceased to be an EU member state, this would depend upon an agreement that amounts to an amendment of the EEA Agreement. Either the UK must join the EFTA and upon this join the EEA Agreement by an agreement of accession to the EEA, or Article 126 of the EEA Agreement must be amended to include the territory of the UK. Under this there would probably have to be agreed an arrangement to include surveillance and jurisdiction over the UK by either the EU or the EFTA institutions.

The question of who would have to agree to such solutions is not altogether clear. The EFTA solution would require the agreement also of Switzerland, since Switzerland is party to the EFTA Treaty. The solution without EFTA membership would only concern the parties to the EEA Agreement. Amending Article 126 is a regular treaty amendment that would have to be undertaken under the normal treaty rules of international public law. The powers of the EEA Joint Committee under Article 98 to amend the treaty do not include amending Article 126. This means that such an amendment lies in the hands of the contracting parties, and not in the institutions of the EEA.

We are thus back to the question of who it is that has the competence on the side of the EU to agree to amendments of the EEA Agreement. If this competence now lies exclusively with the EU under Article 207 TFEU, it is not necessary to include the member states in the procedure of signing and ratification of an agreement to amend. However, the practice within the EU has been, all the way up to the latest amendment in 2014 that included Croatia in the EEA, to include the member states in a mixed-treaty procedure (Official Journal of the European Union, 2014). Given the time constraints in the negotiations, it is safe to assume that the member states will be included in the discussions on the arrangements in order to secure their support.

The legal considerations brought up here have bearing on the nature and ease of the choice of option. In political terms power considerations will figure prominently. For Norway there is a trade-off between predictability and influence. If the UK joins the EEA on a permanent basis, the UK's significantly greater size and global influence will make the EEA very lopsided. The UK's and Norway's differences in interests and priorities will become apparent, as the EEA is not tailored to the UK's interests. The non-EU EEA countries have to agree as one to adopt a Union law into the EEA. This has worked well up until now, but is likely to be much harder should the UK be part of this arrangement.

Norway's Prime Minister Erna Solberg has recently noted that the UK and Norway have different interests in fish, agriculture and labour market standards, among others (Haugan and Andersen, 2017). The UK is also likely to politicise the EEA Agreement and in doing so may render more starkly apparent the fact that EEA countries are not EU members. Norway today enjoys a status within much of the EU as a kind of awkward special arrangement 'member' because it is so tightly included. The process of Brexit will symbolically and substantively underline the non-membership status which will clearly rub off on the EEA if the UK is included. The Norwegian employers' association (NHO) has underlined that it is a great advantage that the UK remains within the EU's internal market but the NHO notes that the UK may weaken the EEA if it joins as a member. A third pillar within the EEA should therefore be established for the UK (Myhre, 2017). Even that may be politicisation-prone though, both internally in Norway and in Norway's relationship to the EU.

Scenario 4: A two-tiered EU with the UK in the outer tier

This scenario underlines that we need to consider Brexit in light of the discussions that are currently unfolding in the EU about further EU consolidation. The EU's crises have exhibited a structural weakness in the eurozone that is only partly addressed.

The effects on Norway from this option hinge to a large extent on the EU's institutional development. There are two main options here. One is for EU core consolidation to entail strengthening the eurozone in terms of better regulations but without major institutional-constitutional reforms or altering the institutional centre of gravity in the EU. We refer to that as *policy and regulatory differentiation*, where policies are differentiated in terms of access/determination. That could still leave scope for non-members (Norway) and ex-members (UK) insofar as the patterns of differentiation did not follow membership lines. After all, this is an important aspect of how Norway has obtained such a close relationship to the EU (in those areas outside the EEA and Schengen). But if membership becomes a criterion, as we see for instance in the newly agreed Permanent Structured Cooperation (PESCO) agreement in the area of defence, and a non-member such as Norway will only have access to single projects and in exceptional circumstances, where the participation of a third country will yield a decisive added value, the potential for exclusion increases.[38]

In some policy areas we might then even face a three-tiered EU: core members (within the eurozone); non-core members (outside the eurozone) but with access to various policies such as PESCO; and non-members. This complex construct would most likely generate pressures for harmonising relations with non-members, which would for instance mean that Norway's relations would be similar to the UK's. The question then is how willing the EU will be to make exceptions and to which countries those may apply. Since the UK weighs in much more heavily in defence than does Norway, the latter may find it very difficult to get its voice heard.

The other option, which we may term *polity differentiation*, refers to core consolidation in institutional-constitutional terms, and an ensuing change in the EU's institutional centre of gravity. That would probably generate a two-tiered structure: core members in the eurozone and outsiders, whether members or not. The European Commission's (2017c) White Paper on EU reform lists five different options, with the third option the one most akin to the notion of a two-tiered EU in polity differentiation terms. An important question is where the EU's closely affiliated non-members and the UK as ex-member will be. Would the non-members be inside or outside the outer tier? An important determining factor would be how strong the divide between tiers would be.

Those in the outer tier would have limited access, and a difficult process of working out their relations with the EU would ensue. It is likely to be a politicised process among the states in the periphery. If they were left outside the two tiers, the non-members could easily be forgotten and lose out on market access. It is therefore reasonable to assume that they would want to be inside the second tier, but even there a state such as Norway would be a small state and could easily find itself at the mercy of cantankerous large states. It is quite obvious that the states in the EU's outer tier would have less in common with Norway – and the UK for that matter – than will the states in the EU's inner core.

Concluding reflections

In this chapter, we have discussed possible effects of Brexit on closely affiliated non-members, with an emphasis on Norway. Brexit opens up a new trilateral dynamic in Norway's relations to its closest trading partners and allies, a dynamic that is driven by them. Norway is not included in the negotiations and will be at the receiving end until the dust has cleared on the EU–UK relationship. There will be strategic considerations as to when to initiate bilateral talks with the UK and on what themes. At present, the Norwegian government is trying to stay abreast with developments and at the same time waiting to see what emanates from the EU–UK negotiations.

We know that the effects of Brexit will be substantial but we cannot tell precisely what they will be because much hinges on the dynamics of the negotiations and the option that the UK ends up with. Critical considerations will be degrees of interest congruity with the EU in respect to the UK; basic patterns of trust (or lack of such); and patterns of politicisation and depoliticisation.

The four different scenarios that we outlined represent different types of challenges. For Norway, the degree of exclusion will vary. It will probably be most pronounced under the first and fourth scenarios: the first because the absence of agreements will generate uncertainty and arbitrariness and systematically favour big states/associations; the fourth because a two-tiered Europe will alter the centre of gravity and lead to more permanent exclusions. The second and third scenarios are closer to the present situation but both will represent significant challenges for Norway.

Conclusion

The purpose of this book was to provide an in-depth assessment of Norway's EU relationship with a view to its suitability to the UK. To that end, we examined what the UK wants; how the EU structures its relations with non-members that seek a close EU affiliation; the nature and range of Norway's EU associations; and how Norway ends up trying to reconcile sovereign control and access. In the last substantive chapter (Chapter Six) we discussed what effects the UK's future EU association might have on Norway, with reference to four different scenarios.

The book has shown that the key actors that currently seek to negotiate the Brexit process, the UK government and its EU counterpart, diverge in their underlying conceptions of what the process is about and how to understand the EU. The UK government, in its attempts at escaping from the web of EU rules and norms currently affecting it, is underlining the need to reach new flexible arrangements through extensive processes of political bargaining across a broad range of issue areas. Conversely, the EU has from the start been concerned about developing and adhering to a set of rules and procedures for how the process should unfold. Thus far, the EU's approach has won out, as is clearly reflected in the Withdrawal Agreement of December 2017. It is notable, however, that this disagreement does not only come down to a different emphasis on how to juxtapose politics and law; the two parties hold quite different perceptions of what the EU is and how it operates.

Even if there are many different conceptions of the EU in the UK, successive UK governments have generally viewed the EU as a single market upheld by a collection of states that have different interests and do not share a common view of political Europe. Thus, Brexit represents an extension – and aggravation – of the UK's traditional role of negotiating its European presence. The challenge, as they see it, is to strike an agreement with the EU's composite membership, which is the EU's member states. The UK government's approach is characteristically statist: the executive is in the driver's seat and all other interests should be aligned accordingly, to the chagrin of much of the UK Parliament, the devolved nations and large sections of the UK business and labour communities.

The EU counterpart exhibits the deeply held notion that the single market is a core vehicle in the development of the EU as a political entity. But whereas the UK and Norway share a deep scepticism of a European federation (as noted in Chapter One), in much of continental Europe it is widely recognised that the EU is a distinct form of federation of nation states. The EU's member states have committed to legally binding cooperation. And despite many disagreements they have created a structure that is far more committing than what would mark a confederation of states. The EU sees Brexit as a form of secession, as a failure to convince the UK to abide by its rules and norms, and treats Brexit in terms similar to how democratic states would do in the contemporary era (a logical parallel here is Canada with its provisions for Quebec secession).

The EU's political vocation and conception of itself as a political system is expressed in its motto 'ever closer union', which also shapes its agreements with non-members. The EU's dynamic approach lends itself to considerable flexibility in the legal arrangements that it signs with third parties. But there are limits, which follow from the CJEU's consistently articulated need to retain the integrity of the EU legal system, the *acquis*. That is why relations with third parties or non-members are not only flexible, they are also in a sense *conditional* on compliance with core EU principles.

Once the UK withdraws, it will not take part in the common goal and purpose of the EU. According to the case law of the CJEU, this may affect the interpretation of the rules, and identically worded rules in the EU and the UK may develop different contents (see Official Journal of the European Communities, 1982). Outside of the EU, the Commission will no longer monitor the adherence to the rules by UK authorities, and authorities in EU countries will no longer be under an obligation to accept certificates and assurances of compliance by UK authorities. The rules on state aid will not apply. This does not mean that the UK will be free to support its industries and businesses in their trade with EU countries: to the contrary, the EU may meet such support with protective measures, and conflicts between the EU and the UK may be governed by WTO rules instead of EU law. There will also be no mechanism for ensuring that as the rules develop within the EU, the rules are changed in the UK. The European Union Withdrawal Bill may create homogeneity between EU and UK law, but it will not provide for this homogeneity to be dynamic. All these factors represent not only political challenges for the UK in the future, but also challenges of an administrative and legal nature.

The short-term prospects

From the presentation of the different range of affiliations with non-members in the preceding chapters, we see that there is no clear, ready-made model that the UK can adopt as its future affiliation with the EU. In the debate, we often see two models contrasted as the 'Swiss model' and the 'Norway model'. In fact, both countries are affiliated to the EU through several models, and both countries have more than 120 agreements each with the EU, which constitute and determine their affiliation. What we see are a range of different arrangements that vary in scope, legal construction, institutional setup and domestic effect. The picture that emerges is one of flexibility and pragmatism, but also with a high degree of complexity and rigidity due to requirements of EU law.

What appears as a model set apart from many of the others is the EEA Agreement. The EEA Agreement is wide-ranging in its scope, but still limited. It has institutional solutions to the issue of how to settle the need for a dynamic cooperation with the EEA Committee and the EFTA Court. The EFTA Surveillance Authority (ESA) provides an arrangement to ensure confidence in that the EFTA countries perform according to their obligations under the agreement. ESA and the court ensure the level of rule of law the EU demands for a state to take part fully in the internal market.

There are other ways of achieving the same objectives. The 'guillotine' clauses of the Swiss agreements and the Schengen agreement provide incentives for keeping up the dynamics of the relationship. Schengen also has a different solution to achieve homogeneity in the application of the agreement by the courts. There is no Schengen court, but the Mixed Committee shall keep under constant review the development of the case law of the Court of Justice of the European Communities, as well as the development of the case law of the competent courts of Iceland and Norway relating to such provisions. Iceland and Norway are entitled to submit statements of case or written observations to the Court of Justice in cases where a question has been referred to it by a court or tribunal of a member state for a preliminary ruling concerning the interpretation of any provision on Schengen. In the case of substantial difference in application between the authorities of the member states concerned and those of Iceland or Norway in respect of the provisions, the Mixed Committee shall try to settle the dispute within 90 days. If this fails, the guillotine is set in action. This is a political mechanism that might presuppose that the number of cases is limited.

Flexibility is also demonstrated in the numerous exceptions from EEA law that are granted, in particular to Liechtenstein. Frommelt distinguishes between opt-outs related to Liechtenstein's smallness and opt-outs related to its close relations with Switzerland (Frommelt 2018, 55-6). The opt-outs are embedded in a narrow institutional corset according to which Liechtenstein cannot take advantage of its opt-outs for its own economic benefit. In particular the opt-outs concerning relations with Switzerland show that special adaptations of an EEA-like arrangement should be possible to accommodate the special conditions between the UK and Ireland. They also demonstrate the limits and constraints that govern special relations within the EEA.

The high degree of complexity in the different affiliations make it inaccurate to speak of 'one model' that can be adopted by the UK, even if there are certain principles and standards that will have to apply to any agreement. The UK will have to find its own form of affiliation with the EU. It is probable, however, that this model will be constructed out of elements that are already known from the different affiliations that we can see between the EFTA countries and the EU.

Considering the time constraint on the on-going Brexit negotiations, we see three likely alternative outcomes in the short term. One is a 'hard' Brexit where the UK leaves the EU without any agreement on a future affiliation. Another is a situation where the UK leaves, but where the whole *acquis* is extended for a period of transition for the parties to hammer out a more permanent solution. A third alternative, where Article 50 is extended beyond the two-year period, is also a possibility that may become more likely as the end date approaches.

Under the two latter 'soft' alternatives, we will be likely to find elements of 'the Norway Model', and more or less clever attempts to disguise their presence. The agreement on the first phase of the negotiation between the EU and the UK already points in this direction. But even if the UK approaches a future relationship with the EU which resembles that of Norway, it is far from certain that this will be explicitly acknowledged. There may be efforts to cloak or conceal that.

To what extent is the Norwegian model transferable?

Brexit suggests that the UK and Norway will be moving in opposite directions. But as this book has shown, there are strong forces in the UK (and the EU) that want some form of assured EU access; hence there are limits to this divergence, especially if the UK continues on its present slide towards some form of 'soft' Brexit. This book has shown that the Norway model is a complex structure, and some of its elements may figure in the arrangements linking the UK to the EU. Nevertheless, when discussing transferability, the issue shifts to internal adoption, acceptance and the UK's ability to live with this form of association. The UK is unlikely to end up balancing state sovereignty, national democracy and market access in a manner similar to Norway. Norway's handling of its many types of EU association relies on a range of factors, not the least the ability to depoliticise the situation and to disassociate the deeply politicised issue of EU membership from the rapid and dynamic process of EU adaptation. We can expect very different politicisation–depoliticisation dynamics in Norway than in the UK, because the UK political system is unlikely to be able to curtail or contain political conflicts in the manner in which Norway has done. The UK's confrontation-prone political system stands in marked contrast to the consensus-seeking Norwegian political system. The Norwegian political system is also marked by a high level of trust in the government and the public sector. That form of trust works as a buffer and makes it easier for the Norwegian government to be considered a trusted EU associate. The UK is very unlikely to emulate Norway on the high level of trust in government. The issue of trust will also figure strongly in the ongoing EU–UK negotiations.

Notes

1 Denmark 1992, and 2015; France 2005; Ireland 2001, 2008; and the Netherlands 2005, as well as other negative referenda in Denmark, Sweden, the Netherlands, Hungary.

2 Speech by Jacques Delors (Luxembourg, 9 September 1985) Bulletin of the European Communities. September 1985, No 9. Luxembourg: Office for official publications of the European Communities. Available at: http://www.cvce.eu/obj/speech_by_jacques_delors_luxembourg_9_september_1985-en-423d6913-b4e2-4395-9157-fe70b3ca8521.html

3 This was discussed in a UK House of Commons Debate on 6 November 2017 (UK Parliament, 2017a).

4 In addition, Wincott (2017, 681) notes that '[b]y September 2016, Whitehall was smaller than it had been since 1939'.

5 Option to opt in to Title IV TEU on visa, asylum, immigration and other policies related to free movement of persons.

6 Opinion 1/91 of the Court of 14 December 1991 on the Draft Agreement between the Community, on the one hand, and the countries of the European Free Trade Association, on the other, relating to the creation of the European Economic Area, Official Journal of the European Communities, 1991 and Opinion 2/13 of the Court (Full Court) of 18 December 2014 of the Draft international agreement – Accession of the European Union to the European Convention for the Protection of Human Rights and Fundamental Freedoms – Compatibility of the Draft Agreement with the EU and FEU Treaties, published in the electronic Reports of Cases (Court Reports – general).

7 Election of 8 June: the Conservative Party got 318 seats (lost 13); Labour got 262 (a gain of 30); SNP got 35 (lost 21); Lib-Dems 12 (a gain of 4); DUP 10 (a gain of 2); UKIP lost its one seat. Source: www.bbc.com/news/election/2017/results/england

8 www.standard.co.uk/news/politics/brexit-philip-hammond-risks-new-cabinet-rift-by-keeping-door-open-to-turkeystyle-deal-a3732811.html

[9] Prior to the June 2017 election there was a 73% majority of Remainers in the House of Commons.

[10] https://publiclawforeveryone.com/2017/07/14/the-eu-withdrawal-bill-initial-thoughts/

[11] The Copenhagen criteria are: (1) stability of institutions guaranteeing democracy, the rule of law, human rights and respect for and protection of minorities; (2) a functioning market economy and the ability to cope with competitive pressure and market forces within the EU; (3) ability to take on the obligations of membership, including the capacity to effectively implement the rules, standards and policies that make up the body of EU law (the *acquis*), and adherence to the aims of political, economic and monetary union. There is an important debate on conditionality in connection with EU enlargement. See for instance Schimmelfennig and Sedelmeier (2004); and Steunenberg and Dimitrova (2007).

[12] The wording of the corresponding provision, Article 1 (2) of the agreement on air transport, is slightly different: 'Insofar as [the regulations and directives] are identical in substance to corresponding rules of the EC Treaty and to acts adopted in application of that Treaty, those provisions shall, in their implementation and application, be interpreted in conformity with the relevant rulings and decisions of the Court of Justice and the Commission of the European Communities given prior to the date of signature of this Agreement. The rulings and decisions given after the date of signature of this Agreement shall be communicated to Switzerland' (Official Journal of the European Communities, 2002b).

[13] See also the speech by C. Baudenbacher (2016), President of the EFTA Court on the EEA option for the United Kingdom after Brexit.

[14] For an overview of the development of EC–EFTA relations as a background to the EEA Agreement see Nordberg and Johansson (2016).

[15] For a comment on this opinion and the subsequent opinion 1/92, see Brandtner (1992, 300f).

[16] On the principle of dynamic homogeneity in EEA law, see Hreinsson (2015).

[17] On the doctrine of direct effect and EEA law in Norway see Bull (1997).

[18] Case E-4/01, *Karlsson v The Icelandic State*: 'It follows from Article 7 EEA and Protocol 35 to the EEA Agreement that EEA law does not entail a transfer of legislative powers. Therefore, EEA law does not require that individuals and economic operators can rely directly on non-implemented EEA rules before national courts' (EFTA Court of Justice, 2002).

[19] For an overview and comparison, see Rosas (2015).

[20] See for a recent example in trademark law, HR-2016-1993-A (Norwegian Supreme Court, 2016).

[21] See Case E-02/11, EFTA Court (2012). See also the presentation of the case given by Barnard (2015).

NOTES

[22] Speech at the Conference of International Courts on their importance for the Norwegian Legal Order, Tromsø, 19 April 2013, translated into Norwegian and published as Baudenbacher (2013).

[23] For an assessment of how the Norwegian political parties have relied on gag rules such as suicide clauses and other types of mechanisms for preventing the EU membership issue from entering the political agenda, see Fossum (2010).

[24] See Morphet (2014) for comments on the cumulative effect of EU law in comparison with the episodic approach to law in the UK).

[25] See for example the EU–Canada Comprehensive Economic and Trade Agreement (CETA) Article 9.3 (1) which states that 'Each Party shall accord to service suppliers and services of the other Party treatment no less favourable than that it accords, in like situations, to its own service suppliers and services' (Council of the European Union, 2016).

[26] In this connection, it is interesting to note that Nicola Sturgeon's Scotland, which seeks to retain access to the EU's single market and thus a differentiated status from the rest of the UK, has a far more favourable view of Norway's EU arrangement than does May's UK government (Government of Scotland, 2016).

[27] See the semi-annual statement to parliament on important EEA and EU issues, delivered by the EU/EEA minister (Røsland, 2017a).

[28] See TFEU, Article 3 (1) (Official Journal of the European Union, 2012).

[29] See Røsland at: www.regjeringen.no/no/dep/ud/org/emin/id2576274/

[30] According to Lovdata (collection of online legal resources), there are 253 treaties between Norway and the UK (Ask, 2017).

[31] These are: Næringslivets hovedorganisasjon (NHO), Landsorganisasjonen i Norge (LO), Yrkesorganisasjonenes sentralforbund (YS), UNIO, Kommunenes sentralforbund (KS), Virke, Norges fiskarlag, Norges bondelag og Norges bonde- og småbrukarlag, Norges rederiforbund, og Finans Norge.

[32] Since the referendum, well over 40 Brexit-related meetings at ministerial level have been held with officials from UK and EU (Bakke-Jensen, 2017b).

[33] www.nytid.no/brutal-brexit-norge/

[34] The European Council conclusions from 15 December 2017 stated its willingness to negotiate a transition period of two years (European Council, 2017).

[35] The relevant principle is loyal cooperation, as stated in Article 4 (3) TEU (Official Journal of the European Union, 2012).

[36] 'In services, CETA allows for some limited mutual recognition of professional qualifications, but there is no general regulatory alignment. There is no requirement on Canada to maintain a level playing field beyond a few general commitments to uphold international standards' (Institute of Government, 2017, 11).

[37] See the references mentioned by Hillion (2018, 958).

[38] 'PESCO is open to all Member States meeting the requirements, and can establish cooperation in five fields: budgetary (setting objectives on the level of investment in defence); equipment (identifying military needs, pooling and sharing, and specialisation); operational (interoperability and readiness of forces); capabilities (remedying the capability gaps) and industry (participating in major equipment programmes)' (European Parliament, 2017).

References

Adler-Nissen, R. (2014) *Opting Out of the European Union*, Cambridge: Cambridge University Press.

Ask, A. O. (2017) 'Hvilke avtaler gjelder etter Brexit? Norge leter på arkivloftet i UD for å finne svaret' (What deals are valid after Brexit? Norway is searching the attic of the foreign office to find the answer), *Aftenposten*, 24 March. Available at: www.aftenposten.no/verden/i/OK6rA/Hvilke-avtaler-gjelder-etter-Brexit-Norge-leter-pa-arkivloftet-i-UD-for-a-finne-svaret

Asthana, A. (2017) 'Parliament to Have "Take-it-or-Leave-it Vote" on Final Brexit Deal, Davis Says', *The Guardian*, 13 November. Available at: www.theguardian.com/politics/2017/nov/13/parliament-to-have-final-say-on-brexit-deal-david-davis-announces

Arnesen, F. (2018) Article 126 (Territorial application of the EEA Agreement) in F. Arnesen, H. Haukeland Fredriksen, H. P. Graver, O. Mæstad and C. Vedder, *Agreement on the European Economic Area A Commentary*, Baden-Baden: Nomos.

Bakke-Jensen, F. (2017a) 'Statement on Norway and Brexit' [Innlegg om Norge og Brexit], speech given at Arendalsuka, 16 August. Available at: www.regjeringen.no/no/aktuelt/innlegg-norge-og-brexit/id2567728/

Bakke-Jensen, F. (2017b) 'Ivaretar norske interesser', (Defending Norwegian Interests) Statement published in *Dagens Næringsliv*, 29 July. Available at: www.regjeringen.no/no/aktuelt/brexit_forberedelser2/id2565105/

Bårdsen, A. (2013) 'Noen Refleksjoner om Norges Høyesterett og EFTA-domstolen' [Some reflections on the Norwegian Supreme Court and the EFTA Court], *Lov og Rett*, 8: 535-46.

Barnard, C. (2015) 'Reciprocity, Homogeneity and Loyal Cooperation: Dealing with Recalcitrant National Courts?', in EFTA Court (ed) *The EEA and the EFTA Court: Decentred Integration*, Oxford: Hart Publishing, pp 151-68.

Bartels, L. (2016) 'The UK's Status in the WTO after Brexit', Paper published in SSRN, 23 September. Available at: https://ssrn.com/abstract=2841747

Baudenbacher, C. (2005) 'The EFTA Court Ten Years On', in C. Baudenbacher, P. Tresselt and T. Örlygsson (eds) *The EFTA Court Ten Years On*, Oxford: Hart Publishing, pp 13-54.

Baudenbacher, C. (2013) 'EFTA-domstolen og dens samhandling med de norske domstolene', (The EFTA Court and the Norwegian Courts) *Lov og Rett*, 8: 515-34.

Baudenbacher, C. (2015) 'The Relationship between the EFTA Court and the Court of Justice of the European Union', in C. Baudenbacher (ed) *The Handbook of EEA Law*, Berlin, Springer International Publishing, pp 179-94.

Baudenbacher, C. (2016) 'After Brexit: Is the EEA an Option for the United Kingdom?', The 42nd Annual Lecture of the Centre for European Law, King's College London, 13 October. Available at http://1exagu1grkmq3k572418odoooym-wpengine.netdna-ssl.com/wp-content/uploads/2016/11/Baudenbacher-Kings-College-13-10-16.pdf

Björgvinsson, D.T. (2014) 'Fundamental Rights in EEA Law', in the EFTA Court (ed) *The EEA and the EFTA Court: Decentred Integration*, Oxford: Hart Publishing, pp 263-79.

Børde, K. (1997) 'The European Economic Area, Norway and the European Union', in P. C. Müller-Graff and E. Selvig (eds) *The European Economic Area – Norway's Basic Status in the Legal Construction of Europe*, Berlin: Berlin Verlag Arno Spitz, pp 97-129.

Brandtner, B. (1992) 'The "Drama" of the EEA: Comments on Opinions 1/91 and 1/92', *European Journal of International Law*, 3 (2): 300–328.

Briggs, M. (2015) 'Europe "à la carte": The Whats and Whys behind UK Opt-outs', *Euractiv*, 7 May. Available at: www.euractiv.com/section/uk-europe/linksdossier/europe-a-la-carte-the-whats-and-whys-behind-uk-opt-outs/

Bull, H. (1997) 'European Law and Norwegian Courts', in P. C. Müller-Graff and E. Selvig (eds) *The Approach to European Law in Germany and Norway*, Berlin: Berliner Wissenschafts-Verlag, pp 95–114.

Burke, C., Hannesson, Ó. Í. and Bangsund, K. (2016) 'Life on the Edge: EFTA and the EEA as a Future for the UK in Europe', *European Public Law*, 22 (1): 69–96.

Council of the European Union (2016) Comprehensive Economic and Trade Agreement (CETA) Between Canada, of the One Part, and the European Union of the Other Part, 10973/16.

Dagens Næringsliv (2017) 'Erna Solberg Invitert med på Eksklusivt Brexitmøte', (Prime Minister Erna Solberg invited to an exclusive Brexit meeting) *Dagens Næringsliv*, 19 October. Available at: www.dn.no/nyheter/2017/10/19/0607/Politikk/erna-solberg-invitert-med-pa-eksklusivt-brexitmote

Defeis, E. (2012) 'Human Rights, the European Union, and the Treaty Route: From Maastricht to Lisbon', *Fordham International Law Journal*, 35 (5): 1207–30.

Dystland, M. K. F., Finstad, F. B., and Sørebø, I. (2018) 'Article 102 (Amendments of Annexes, incorporation of EEA-relevant EU legislation', in F. Arnesen, H. Haukeland Fredriksen, H. P. Graver, O. Mæstad and C. Vedder, *Agreement on the European Economic Area A Commentary*, Baden-Baden: Nomos.

Eeckhout, P. and Patel, O. (2017) 'Brexit Transitional Arrangements: Legal and Political Considerations', *UCL European Institute, Brexit Insights*, November, 1–15.

EFTA (2017) 'The Basic Features of the EEA Agreement'. Available at www.efta.int/eea/eea-agreement/eea-basic-features#1

EFTA Court of Justice (1997) Advisory Opinion of the Court, 3 December 1997. *Fridtjof Frank Gundersen v Oslo Municipality (supported by the Government of the Kingdom of Norway)*. Case E-01/97.

EFTA Court of Justice (1998) Advisory Opinion of the Court, 10 December 1998. *Erla María Sveinbjörnsdóttir v Government of Iceland*. Case E-9/97.

EFTA Court of Justice (2002) Judgment of the Court, 30 May 2002. *Karl K. Karlsson hf. v Republic of Iceland*. Case E-4/01.

EFTA Court of Justice (2011) Report for the hearing in Case E-12/10. *EFTA Surveillance Authority v Iceland*. Case E-12/10.

EFTA Court of Justice (2012) Judgment of the Court, 31 January 2012. *STX Norway Offshore AS and others v the Norwegian State, represented by the Tariff Board*. Case E-02/11.

EFTA Court of Justice (2013) *The Norwegian State, represented by the Ministry of Labour v Stig Arne Jonsson*. Case E-3/12.

Elliott, L. (2016) 'WTO Chief Says Post-Brexit Trade Talks Must Start From Scratch', *The Guardian*, 7 June. Available at: www.theguardian.com/business/2016/jun/07/wto-chief-brexit-trade-talks-start-scratch-eu-referendum

Elliott, M. (2017) 'The EU (Withdrawal) Bill: Initial Thoughts', *Public Law for Everyone*, 14 July. Available at: https://publiclawforeveryone.com/2017/07/14/the-eu-withdrawal-bill-initial-thoughts/

Eriksen, E. O. and Fossum J. E. (eds) (2015) *The European Union's Non-members: Independence under Hegemony?*, London: Routledge.

European Commission (2017a) 'Joint Report from the Negotiations of the European Union and the United Kingdom Government on Progress During Phase 1 of Negotiations Under Article 50 TEU on the United Kingdom's Orderly Withdrawal from the European Union', TF50 (2017) 19, 9 December. Available at: https://ec.europa.eu/commission/sites/beta-political/files/joint_report.pdf

European Commission (2017b) 'Speech by Michel Barnier at the Centre for European Reform on "The Future of the EU"', Brussels, 20 November. Available at: http://europa.eu/rapid/press-release_SPEECH-17-4765_en.htm

European Commission (2017c) 'White Paper on the Future of Europe: Reflections and Scenarios for the EU27 by 2025', 1 March. Available at: https://ec.europa.eu/commission/sites/beta-political/files/white_paper_on_the_future_of_europe_en.pdf

European Council (2017) 'European Council (Art. 50) meeting (15 December 2017) Guidelines', EUCO XT 20011/17, BXT 69 CO EUR 27 CONCL 8, Brussels, 15 December. Available at: www.consilium.europa.eu/media/32236/15-euco-art50-guidelines-en.pdf

European Parliament (2017) 'Permanent Structured Cooperation (PESCO): From Notification to Establishment', *At a Glance*, December. Available at: www.europarl.europa.eu/EPRS/EPRS-AaG-614632-Permanent-structured-cooperation-PESCO-FINAL.pdf

Featherstone, K. (2017) 'The EU and its Neighbours: Reconciling Market Access, Governance and Democracy', *Dahrendorf Forum*, 1 September. Available at: www.dahrendorf-forum.eu/wp-content/uploads/2017/09/Featherstone-Neighbours.pdf

Fløistad, K. (2004) *Fundamental Rights and the EEA Agreement*, ARENA Report Series 04/1, Oslo: ARENA, University of Oslo.

Ford, R. (2017) 'The New Electoral Map of Britain: From the Revenge of Remainers to the Uphending of Class Politics', *The Guardian*, 11 June. Available at: www.theguardian.com/politics/2017/jun/11/new-electoral-map-for-britain-revenge-of-remainers-to-upending-class-politics

Fossum, J. E. (2010) 'Norway's European "Gag Rules"', *European Review*, 18 (1): 73–92.

Fossum, J. E. (2015) 'Representation Under Hegemony? On Norway's Relationship to the EU', in E. O. Eriksen and J. E. Fossum (eds) *The European Union's Non-members: Independence under Hegemony?*, London: Routledge, pp 153–72.

Fossum, J. E. (2016) 'Norwegian Reflections on Brexit', *Political Quarterly*, 87 (3): 343–47.

Fossum, J. E. and C. Holst. (2014) 'Norsk Konstitusjonell Debatt og Europeisk Integrasjon' (Constitutional debate in Norway and European integration), in E. O. Eriksen and J.-E. Fossum (eds) *Det Norske Paradoks: Om Norges Forhold Til Den Europeiske Union*, Oslo: Universitetsforlaget, pp 196-219.

Fowles, S. (2017) 'The Great Repeal Bill: Addressing Unaccountable Power', *Another Europe is Possible*, briefing paper. Available at: www.anothereurope.org/wp-content/uploads/2017/03/aeip_grb_briefing_web.pdf

Fredriksen, H. H. (2010) 'The EFTA Court Fifteen Years On', *International and Comparative Law Quarterly*, 59 (3): 731-60.

Fredriksen, H. H. (2013) 'Betydningen av EUs Pakt om Grunnleggende Rettigheter for EØS 'Retten', (The implications of the EU Charter on Fundamental Rights on the EEA Agreement)*Jussens Venner*, 48: 371-99.

Fredriksen, H. H. (2015) 'The EEA and the Case Law of the EU of the CJEU: Incorporation without Participation', in E. O. Eriksen and J. E. Fossum (eds) *The European Union's Non-Members: Independence under Hegemony?*, Abingdon: Routledge, pp 102-17.

Fredriksen, H. H. and Franklin, C. N. K. (2015) 'Of Pragmatism and Principles: The EEA Agreement 20 Years On', *Common Market Law Review*, 52 (3): 629-84.

Frommelt, C. (2016) 'Liechtenstein's Tailor-made Arrangements in the EEA: A Small State's Creative Solutions in European Integration', in S. Wolf (ed) *State Size Matters*, Wiesbaden: VS Springer, pp 131-62.

Frommelt, C. (2018) 'Lichtenstein and the EEA', in F. Arnesen, H. Haukeland Fredriksen, H. P. Graver, O. Mæstad and C. Vedder (eds), *Agreement on the European Economic Area A Commentary*, Baden-Baden: Nomos.

Genschel, P. and Jachtenfuchs, M. (eds) (2014) *Beyond the Regulatory Polity? The European Integration of Core State Powers*, Oxford: Oxford University Press.

Gormley-Heenan, C. and Aughey, A. (2017) 'Northern Ireland and Brexit: Three Effects on "the Border in the Mind"', *British Journal of Politics and International Relations*, 19 (3): 497-511.

Government of Scotland (2016) 'Scotland's Place in Europe'. Available at: www.gov.scot/Resource/0051/00512073.pdf

Graver, H. P. (2002) 'Mission Impossible: Supranationality and National Legal Autonomy in the EEA Agreement', *European Foreign Affairs Review*, 7 (1): 73-90.

Gstöhl, S. (2015) 'The European Union's Different Neighbourhood Models', in E. O. Eriksen and J. E. Fossum (eds) *The European Union's Non-members: Independence under Hegemony?*, London: Routledge, pp 17-35.

Guerrina, R. and Masselot, A. (2018) 'Walking into the Footprint of EU Law: Unpacking the Gendered Consequences of Brexit', *Journal of Social Policy and Society*, 17 (2) 319-330.

Hansen, R. (2017) Brexit – Hva Blir Veien Videre?', (Brexit – What is the next step?) *LO*, 10 January. Available at: www.lo.no/Brussel/Temarapporter/Brexit--hva-blir-veien-videre/

Haugan, B. and Andersen, C. S. (2017) 'Erna Kritisk til Britisk EFTA-flørt', (Erna (the PM) Critical to the British EFTA advance) *VG*, 4 September. Available at: www.vg.no/nyheter/innenriks/stortingsvalget-2017/erna-kritisk-til-britisk-efta-floert/a/24132537/

Hillion, C. (2018) 'Article 127 (Withdrawal from the EEA Agreement)', in F. Arnesen, H. Haukeland Fredriksen, H. P. Graver, O. Mæstad and C. Vedder, *Agreement on the European Economic Area A Commentary*, Baden-Baden: Nomos.

Holmes, S. (1995) *Passions and Constraint*, Chicago: Chicago University Press.

Hreinsson, P. (2015) 'General Principles', in C. Baudenbacher (ed) *The Handbook of EEA Law*, Springer International Publishing, pp 349-389. DOI: 10.1007/978-3-319-24343-6_19

Hunt, J. and Minto, R. (2017) 'Between Intergovernmental Relations and Paradiplomacy: Wales and the Brexit of the Regions', *British Journal of Politics and International Relations*, 19(4): 647-62.

Institute for Government (2017) Trade after Brexit - Options for the UK's Relationship with the EU, December 2017. Available at: www.google.no/url?sa=t&rct=j&q=&esrc=s&source=web&cd=1&cad=rja&uact=8&ved=0ahUKEwj82NfZuYrZAhUBFiwKHSOaAEIQFggnMAA&url=https%3A%2F%2Fwww.instituteforgovernment.org.uk%2Fpublications%2Ftrade-after-brexit&usg=AOvVaw0q8j4H4D-Mf0aL8c7V1oWE

Kaddous, C. (2014) '§ 20 Die Zusammenarbeit zwischen der EU und der Schweiz', (The cooperation between the EU and Switzerland) in A. Hatje and P.-C. Müller-Graff (eds) *Europäisches Organisations- und Verfassungsrecht*, Baden-Baden: Nomos, pp 937-84.

Keating, M. (2001) *Plurinational Democracy – Stateless Nations in a Post-Sovereignty Era*, Oxford: Oxford University Press.

Lavenex, S. (2009) 'Switzerland's Flexible Integration in the EU: A Conceptual Framework', *Swiss Political Science Review*, 15 (4): 547-76.

Lavenex, S. and Schwok, R. (2015) 'The Nature of Switzerland's Relationship with the EU', in E.O. Eriksen and J.E. Fossum (eds) *The European Union's Non-Members: Independence under Hegemony?*, London: Routledge, pp 36-51.

Lavery, S. (2017) '"Defend and Extend": British Business Strategy, EU Employment Policy and the Emerging Politics of Brexit', *British Journal of Politics and International Relations*, 19 (4): 696-714.

Lord, C. (2015) 'The United Kingdom, a Once and Future (?) Non-Member State', in E. O. Eriksen and J. E. Fossum (ed.), *The European Union's Non-members: Independence under Hegemony?*, London: Routledge, pp 211-29.

Magnusson, S. (2014) 'Efficient Judicial Protection of EEA Rights in the EFTA Pillar – Different Role for the National Judge?', in EFTA Court (ed) *The EEA and the EFTA Court: Decentred Integration*, Oxford: Hart Publishing, pp 117-32.

May, T. (2017) 'The Government's Negotiating Objectives for Exiting the EU', Speech delivered in Lancaster House, London, 17 January. Available at: www.gov.uk/government/speeches/the-governments-negotiating-objectives-for-exiting-the-eu-pm-speech

Meld.St.36 [White Paper] (2016-2017) 'Setting the Course for Norwegian Foreign and Security Policy', Recommendation from the Ministry of Foreign Affairs approved in the Council, 21 April. Available at: www.regjeringen.no/en/dokumenter/meld.-st.-36-20162017/id2549828/

Morgan, G. (2005) *The Idea of a European Superstate*, Princeton, NJ: Princeton University Press.

Morphet, J. (2014) *How Europe Shapes British Public Policy*, Bristol: Bristol University Press.

Morphet, J. and Clifford, T. (2018) '"Who Else Would We Speak To?" National Policy Networks in Post-devolution Britain: The Case of Spatial Planning', *Public Policy and Administration*, 33 (1): 3-21.

Muirhead, R. (2014) *The Promise of Party in a Polarized Age*, Boston, MA: Harvard University Press.

Murphy, J. (2017) 'Britain Would Do Better to "Soften" Brexit Demands, Says Senior MEP', *Evening Standard*, 22 June. Available at: www.standard.co.uk/news/politics/britain-would-do-better-to-soften-brexit-demands-says-senior-mep-a3570876.html

Myhre, T. (2017) 'En Tredje EØS-vei for Storbritannia?', (A third EEA-way for Great Britain) *NHO*, 18 August. Available at: www.nho.no/Politikk-og-analyse/Internasjonalt/en-tredje-eos-vei-for-storbritannia/

Norberg, S. and Johansson, M. (2016) 'The History of the EEA Agreement and the First Twenty Years of Its Existence', in C. Baudenbacher (ed) *The Handbook of EEA Law*, Zürich: Springer, pp 3-42.

Norwegian Supreme Court (2000) Judgment of the Court, 16 November 2000. *Storebrand Skadeforsikring AS v Veronika Finanger*. HR-2000-49-B - Rt-2000-1811.

Norwegian Supreme Court (2005) Judgment of the Court, 28 October 2005. *Veronika Finanger v the State, by the Ministry of Justice*. HR-2005-1690-P - Rt-2005-1365.

Norwegian Supreme Court (2013) Judgment of the Court, 5 March. *STX Norway Offshore AS and others v the Norwegian State, by the Tariff Board*. HR-2013-496-A - Rt-2013-258.

Norwegian Supreme Court (2016) Judgment of the Court, 22 September 2016. *Pangea Property Partners AS v the State, by Norwegian Board of Appeal for Industrial Property Rights.* HR-2016-1993-A.

NOU 2012:2 [Norwegian Official Report] (2012) 'Outside and Inside: Norway's Agreements with the European Union', Report by the EEA Review Committee delivered to the Norwegian Ministry of Foreign Affairs, 17 January. Available at: www.regjeringen.no/no/dokumenter/nou-2012-2/id669368/

Official Journal of the European Communities (1982) Judgment of the Court of 9 February 1982. *Polydor Limited and RSO Records Inc. v Harlequin Records Shops Limited and Simons Records Limited.* Case 270/80.

Official Journal of the European Communities (1991) Opinion pursuant to Article 228 of the EEC Treaty. Opinion 1/91, 14 December.

Official Journal of the European Communities (1994a) Agreement between the EFTA States on the Establishment of a Surveillance Authority and a Court of Justice. L 344/1, 31 December.

Official Journal of the European Communities (1994b) Agreement on the European Economic Area. OJ L 1, 3 January.

Official Journal of the European Communities (1999) Council Decision of 17 May 1999 on Certain Arrangements for the Application of the Agreement Concluded by the Council of the European Union and the Republic of Iceland and the Kingdom of Norway Concerning the Association of Those Two States with the Implementation, Application and Development of the Schengen Acquis. L 176/31, 10 July.

Official Journal of the European Communities (2001) Council Decision of 15 March 2001 Concerning the Conclusion of an Agreement Between the European Community and the Republic of Iceland and the Kingdom of Norway Concerning the Criteria and Mechanisms for Establishing the State Responsible for Examining a Request for Asylum Lodged in a Member State or Iceland or Norway. L 93, 3 April.

Official Journal of the European Communities (2002a) Agreement Between the European Community and its Member States, of the One Part, and the Swiss Confederation, of the Other, on the Free Movement of Persons. L 114/6, 30 April.

Official Journal of the European Communities (2002b) Agreement Between the European Community and the Swiss Confederation on Air Transport. L 114/73, 30 April.

Official Journal of the European Communities (2003) Judgment of the Court of 23 September 2003. *Margarethe Ospelt and Schlössle Weissenberg Familienstiftung*. Case C-452/01.

Official Journal of the European Union (2009) Judgment of the Court (Fourth Chamber) of 12 November 2009. *Christian Grimme v Deutsche Angestellten-Krankenkasse*. Case C-351/08.

Official Journal of the European Union (2010) Judgment of the Court (Third Chamber) of 11 February 2010. *Fokus Invest AG v Finanzierungsberatung-Immobilientreuhand und Anlageberatung GmbH (FIAG)*. Case C-541/08.

Official Journal of the European Union (2012) Consolidated versions of the Treaty on European Union and the Treaty on the Functioning of the European Union. C 326.

Official Journal of the European Union (2013) Judgment of the Court (Third Chamber) of 7 March 2013. Case C-547/10 P.

Official Journal of the European Union (2014) Agreement on the Participation of the Republic of Croatia in the European Economic Area and Three Related Agreements. L 170, 11 June.

Olsen, J. P. (2017) *Democratic Accountability, Political Order, and Change*, Oxford: Oxford University Press.

Parker, G. and Pickard, J. (2017) 'UK Has No Plan B if Brexit Fails, Insists Boris Johnson', *Financial Times*, 11 July. Available at: www.ft.com/content/303c3aa0-6655-11e7-8526-7b38dcaef614

Piris, J.-C. (2017) 'Why the UK Will Not Become an EEA Member after Brexit'. Available at: https://esharp.eu/debates/the-uk-and-europe/why-the-uk-will-not-become-an-eea-member-after-brexit

Renwick, A. (2017) 'The Process of Brexit: What Comes Next?', *UCL Working Paper*, January. Available at: www.ucl.ac.uk/constitution-unit/news/the-process-of-brexit

Rodgers, J. (2017) 'A-ha! Tory Candidate Accidentally Embodies Alan Partridge in Embarrassing Election Video', *Express*, 6 June. Available at: www.express.co.uk/news/politics/813524/General-election-Conservative-Sir-Greg-Knight-campaign-video

Rodrik, D. (2011) *The Globalization Paradox: Democracy and the Future of the World Economy*, Oxford: Oxford University Press.

Rosas, A. (2015) 'The Content of Requests for Preliminary Rulings to the European Court of Justice and the EFTA Court – What Are the Minimum Requirements?', in EFTA Court (ed) *The EEA and the EFTA Court: Decentred Integration*, Oxford: Hart Publishing, pp 83-94.

Røsland, M. B. (2017a) 'Semi-annual Statement to Parliament on Important EEA and EU Issues' [Halvårlig Redegjørelse om Viktige EØS- og EU-saker], *Regjeringen.no*, 23 November. Available at: www.regjeringen.no/no/aktuelt/redegjorelse_171123/id2579707/

Røsland, M.B. (2017b) 'Norway in Europe' [EØS- og EU-minister Marit Berger Røslands innlegg under møtet med EU-ambassadørene i Norge], 27 November.

Schimmelfennig, F. and Sedelmeier, U. (2004) 'Governance by Conditionality: EU Rule Transfer to the Candidate Countries of Central and Eastern Europe', *Journal of Euopean Public Policy*, 11 (4): 661-79.

Sejersted, F. (1997) 'Between Sovereignty and Supranationalism in the EEA Context', in P.-C. Müller-Graff and E. Selvig (eds) *The European Economic Area – Norway's Basic Status in the Legal Construction of Europe*, Berlin: Berlin Verlag Arno Spitz, pp 43-73.

Sjursen, H. (2014) 'Demokrati eller Handlingskapasitet? Paradokser i Norges Tilknytning til EU på det Utenriks- og Sikkerhetspolitiske Området', (Democracy or capacity to act? Paradokses in Norway's relations to the EU in the field of defense and security policy) in E. O. Eriksen and J. E. Fossum (eds) *Det Norske Paradoks: Om Norges Forhold til Den Europeiske Union*, Oslo: Universitetsforlaget, pp 174-12.

Sjursen, H. (2015) 'Reinforcing Executive Dominance: Norway and the EU's Foreign and Security Policy', in E. O. Eriksen and J. E. Fossum (eds) *The European Union's Non-members: Independence under Hegemony?*, London: Routledge, pp 189-208.

Stavang, P. (2002) *Parlamentarisme og Folkestyre* (Parliamentarism and popular rule) (4th edn), Bergen: Fagbokforlaget.

Steunenberg, B. and Dimitrova, A. (2007) 'Compliance in the EU Enlargement Process: The Limits of Conditionality', *European Integration Online Papers*, 11: 1-18.

Stewart, H. (2017) 'Brexit: Workers' Rights Best Secured by Staying in Single Market, Says TUC Chief', *The Guardian*, 11 September. Available at: www.theguardian.com/politics/2017/sep/11/brexit-workers-rights-best-secured-by-staying-in-single-market-says-tuc-chief

Tovias, A. (2006) 'Exploring the "Pros" and "Cons" of Swiss and Norwegian Models of Relations with the European Union: What Can Israel Learn from the Experiences of These Two Countries?', *Cooperation and Conflict*, 41 (2): 203-22.

UK Government (2016) 'Alternatives to Membership: Possible Models for the United Kingdom Outside the European Union'. Available at: www.gov.uk/government/uploads/system/uploads/attachment_data/file/504604/Alternatives_to_membership_-_possible_models_for_the_UK_outside_the_EU.pdf

UK Government (2017a) 'The Repeal Bill. Factsheet 1: General', *Department for Exiting the European Union*. Available at: www.gov.uk/government/uploads/system/uploads/attachment_data/file/627983/General_Factsheet.pdf

UK Government (2017b) 'The United Kingdom's Exit from and New Partnership with the European Union', *White Paper*, Cm 9417, 2 February. Available at: www.gov.uk/government/uploads/system/uploads/attachment_data/file/589191/The_United_Kingdoms_exit_from_and_partnership_with_the_EU_Web.pdf

UK Government (2017c) 'Security, Law Enforcement and Criminal Justice, A Future Partnership Paper', 18 September. Available at: www.gov.uk/government/uploads/system/uploads/attachment_data/file/645416/Security__law_enforcement_and_criminal_justice_-_a_future_partnership_paper.PDF

UK Government (2017d) 'Prime Minister's Letter to Donald Tusk Triggering Article 50', 29 March. Available at: www.gov.uk/government/uploads/system/uploads/attachment_data/file/604079/Prime_Ministers_letter_to_European_Council_President_Donald_Tusk.pdf

UK Government (2017e) 'Foreign Policy, Defence and Development: A Future Partnership Paper', 12 September. Available at: www.gov.uk/government/uploads/system/uploads/attachment_data/file/643924/Foreign_policy__defence_and_development_paper.pdf

UK Government (2017f) 'PM's Florence Speech: A New Era of Cooperation and Partnership between the UK and the EU', 22 September. Available at: www.gov.uk/government/speeches/pms-florence-speech-a-new-era-of-cooperation-and-partnership-between-the-uk-and-the-eu

UK Parliament (2017a) 'European Economic Area: UK Membership', *House of Commons Hansard*, 6 November, Vol 630. Available at: https://hansard.parliament.uk/Commons/2017-11-06/debates/FEEE4AD5-7465-47A4-97CA-A9B41B9DCAD9/EuropeanEconomicAreaUKMembership

UK Parliament (2017b) 'European Union (Withdrawal) Bill', House of Commons Research briefing. Available at: http://researchbriefings.parliament.uk/ResearchBriefing/Summary/CBP-8079

REFERENCES

UK Supreme Court (2017a) Judgment *R (on the application of Miller and another) (Respondents) v Secretary of State for Exiting the European Union (Appellant)*, Hilary Term [2017] UKSC 5.

UK Supreme Court (2017b) Press Summary, 24 January. *R (on the application of Miller and another) (Respondents) v Secretary of State for Exiting the European Union (Appellant)*. Available at: www.supremecourt.uk/cases/docs/uksc-2016-0196-press-summary.pdf

Vahl, M. and Grolimund, N. (2006) *Integration without Membership: Switzerland's Bilateral Agreements with the European Union*, Brussels: Centre for European Policy Studies.

Vedder, C. (2018) 'The EEA in the Union's Legal Order', in F. Arnesen, H. Haukeland Fredriksen, H. P. Graver, O. Mæstad and C. Vedder, *Agreement on the European Economic Area A Commentary*, Baden-Baden: Nomos.

Wahl, N. (2014) 'Uncharted Waters? The Charter and EEA Law', in EFTA Court (ed) *The EEA and the EFTA Court: Decentred Integration*, Oxford: Hart Publishing, pp 281-98.

Walker, P., Elgot, J. and Mason, R. (2017) 'Labour Conference Votes to Back Party's Official Policy on Brexit', *The Guardian*, 25 September. Available at: www.theguardian.com/politics/2017/sep/25/john-mcdonnell-labour-members-didnt-want-to-split-party-on-brexit

Wincott, D. (2017) 'Brexit Dilemmas: New Opportunities and Tough Choices in Unsettled Times', *The British Journal of Politics and International Relations*, 19 (4): 680-95.

Zielonka, J. (2006) *Europe as Empire: The Nature of the Enlarged European Union*, Oxford: Oxford University Press.

Appendix

The agreements between the EU and Switzerland from Bilateral I to the present date are:

13/04/2016 Participation Agreement between the European Union and the Swiss Confederation on the participation of the Swiss Confederation in the European Union Advisory Mission for Civilian Security Sector Reform in Ukraine (EUAM Ukraine)

13/04/2016 Participation Agreement between the European Union and the Swiss Confederation on the participation of the Swiss Confederation in the European Union CSDP mission in Mali (EUCAP Sahel Mali)

05/12/2014 Agreement for scientific and technological cooperation between the European Union and European Atomic Energy Community and the Swiss Confederation associating the Swiss Confederation to Horizon 2020 – the Framework Programme for Research and Innovation and the Research and Training Programme of the European Atomic Energy Community complementing Horizon 2020, and regulating the Swiss Confederation's participation in the ITER activities carried out by Fusion for Energy

10/06/2014 Arrangement between the European Union and the Swiss Confederation on the modalities of its participation in the European Asylum Support Office

18/12/2013 Cooperation Agreement between the European Union and its Member States, of the one part, and the Swiss Confederation, of the other, on the European Satellite Navigation Programmes (★)

19/03/2010 Agreement between the European Community and the Republic of Iceland, the Kingdom of Norway, the Swiss Confederation and the Principality of Liechtenstein on supplementary rules in relation to the External Borders Fund for the period 2007 to 2013 (★)

15/02/2010 Agreement between the European Union and the Swiss Confederation establishing the terms and conditions for the participation of the Swiss Confederation in the 'Youth in Action' programme and in the action programme in the field of lifelong learning (2007–2013)

25/06/2009 Agreement between the European Community and the Swiss Confederation on the simplification of inspections and formalities in respect of the carriage of goods and on customs security measures

14/05/2009 Agreement between the European Community and the Swiss Confederation amending the Agreement between the European Community and the Swiss Confederation on trade in agricultural products

29/07/2008 Agreement between the European Union and the Swiss Confederation on the participation of the Swiss Confederation in the European Union Rule of Law Mission in Kosovo, EULEX KOSOVO

28/04/2008 Agreement between the Swiss Confederation and the European Union on the security procedures for the exchange of classified information

11/10/2007 Agreement between the European Community and the Swiss Confederation in the audiovisual field, establishing the terms and conditions for the participation of the Swiss Confederation in the Community programme MEDIA 2007

25/06/2007 Agreement on scientific and technological cooperation between the European Community and the European Atomic Energy Community, of the one part, and the Swiss Confederation, of the other part

22/12/2006 Agreement revising the Agreement between the European Community and the Swiss Confederation on mutual recognition in relation to conformity assessment

10/08/2006 Agreement in the form of an Exchange of Letters between the European Union and the Government of the Swiss Confederation on the participation of the Swiss Confederation in the European Union military operation in support of the United Nations Organisation Mission in the Democratic Republic of the Congo (MONUC) during the election process (Operation EUFOR RD Congo)

22/12/2005 Agreement between the European Union and the Swiss Confederation on the participation of the Swiss Confederation in the European Union Monitoring Mission in Aceh (Indonesia) (Aceh Monitoring Mission - AMM)

22/12/2004 Agreement between the European Union and the Swiss Confederation on the participation of the Swiss Confederation in the European Union military crisis management operation in Bosnia and Herzegovina (operation ALTHEA)

26/10/2004 Agreement between the European Community and the Swiss Confederation amending the agreement between the European Economic Community and the Swiss Confederation of 22 July 1972 concerning the provisions applicable to the processed agricultural products

26/10/2004 Agreement between the European Community and the Swiss Confederation concerning the criteria and mechanisms for establishing the State responsible for examining a request for asylum lodged in a Member State or in Switzerland

26/10/2004 Agreement between the European Community and the Swiss Confederation concerning the participation of Switzerland in the European Environment Agency and the European Environment Information and Observation Network

26/10/2004 Agreement between the European Community and the Swiss Confederation envisaging measures equivalent to those provided for in Council Directive 2003/48/EC on taxation of the incomes of the saving in the form of payments of interests – Memorandum of understanding

26/10/2004 Agreement between the European Community and the Swiss Confederation in the audiovisual field, establishing the terms and conditions for the participation of the Swiss Confederation in the Community programmes MEDIA Plus and MEDIA Training – Final Act – Declarations

26/10/2004 Agreement between the European Community and the Swiss Confederation on cooperation in the field of statistics

26/10/2004 Agreement between the European Union, the European Community and the Swiss Confederation on the Swiss Confederation's association with the implementation, application and development of the Schengen *acquis*

26/10/2004 Agreement in the form of exchange of letters between the European Community and the Swiss Confederation on the date of implementation of the agreement between the European Community and the Swiss Confederation envisaging measures equivalent to those provided for in Council Directive 2003/48/ EC of 3 June 2003 on taxation of the incomes of the saving in the form of payments of interest

26/10/2004 Cooperation Agreement between the European Community and its Member States, of the one part, and the Swiss Confederation, of the other part, to combat fraud and any other illegal activity to the detriment of their financial interests

25/02/2004 Administrative arrangement in the form of exchange of letters between the European Community and the Swiss Confederation concerning the temporary point system applicable to the heavy goods vehicles which cross Austria

21/06/1999 Agreement between the European Community and its Member States, of the one part, and the Swiss Confederation, of the other, on the free movement of persons

21/06/1999 Agreement between the European Community and the Swiss Confederation on Air Transport

21/06/1999 Agreement between the European Community and the Swiss Confederation on certain aspects of government procurement

21/06/1999 Agreement between the European Community and the Swiss Confederation on mutual recognition in relation to conformity assessment

21/06/1999 Agreement between the European Community and the Swiss Confederation on the Carriage of Goods and Passengers by Rail and Road

21/06/1999 Agreement between the European Community and the Swiss Confederation on trade in agricultural products

21/06/1999 Agreement on Scientific and Technological Cooperation between the European Communities and the Swiss Confederation

Source: European External Action Service Treaties Office Database.

The agreements subsequent to and in addition to the EEA Agreement are:

08/12/2016 Agreement between the European Union and the Kingdom of Norway on supplementary rules in relation to the instrument for financial support for external borders and visa, as part of the Internal Security Fund for the period 2014 to 2020

03/05/2016 Agreement between the Kingdom of Norway and the European Union on a Norwegian Financial Mechanism for the period 2014–2021

15/01/2015 Agreement between the European Union and the Kingdom of Norway on reciprocal access to fishing in the Skagerrak for vessels flying the flag of Denmark, Norway and Sweden

22/09/2010 Cooperation Agreement on Satellite Navigation between the European Union and its Member States and the Kingdom of Norway

28/07/2010 Agreement between the Kingdom of Norway and the European Union on a Norwegian Financial Mechanism for the period 2009-2014

19/03/2010 Agreement between the European Community and the Republic of Iceland, the Kingdom of Norway, the Swiss Confederation and the Principality of Liechtenstein on supplementary rules in relation to the External Borders Fund for the period 2007 to 2013

03/05/2016 Agreement between the European Union, Iceland, the Principality of Liechtenstein and the Kingdom of Norway on an EEA Financial Mechanism 2014-2021

28/07/2010 Agreement between the European Union, Iceland, the Principality of Liechtenstein and the Kingdom of Norway on an EEA Financial Mechanism 2009-2014

28/06/2006 Agreement between the European Union and the Republic of Iceland and the Kingdom of Norway on the surrender procedure between the Member States of the European Union and Iceland and Norway - Declarations

09/06/2006 Multilateral Agreement between the European Community and its Member States, the Republic of Albania, Bosnia and Herzegovina, the Republic of Bulgaria, the Republic of Croatia, the former Yugoslav Republic of Macedonia, the Republic of Iceland, the Republic of Montenegro, the Kingdom of Norway, Romania, the Republic of Serbia and the United Nations Interim Administration Mission in Kosovo on the establishment of a European Common Aviation Area

14/12/2006 Agreement between the European Community and the Kingdom of Norway on the revision of the amount of the financial contribution from Norway provided for in the Agreement between the European Community and the Kingdom of Norway on the participation of Norway in the work of the European Monitoring Centre for Drugs and Drug Addiction (EMCDDA)

08/12/2006 Agreement in the form of an Exchange of Letters between the European Community and the Kingdom of Norway concerning adjustments of trade preferences in cheese undertaken on the basis of Article 19 of the Agreement on the European Economic Area

03/12/2004 Agreement between the European Union and the Kingdom of Norway establishing a framework for the participation of the Kingdom of Norway to the crisis management operations led by the European Union – Statements

22/11/2004 Agreement between the European Union and the Kingdom of Norway on the safety procedures for the exchange of classified information

14/10/2003 Agreement between the Kingdom of Norway and the European Community pertaining to a Norwegian financial mechanism for the period 2004–2009

14/10/2003 Agreement in the form of exchange of letters between the European Community and the Kingdom of Norway pertaining to certain products of agriculture

20/06/2003 Agreement in the form of exchange of letters between the European Community and the Kingdom of Norway concerning the granting of additional trade preferences for agricultural products, on the basis of Article 19 of the agreement on the European Economic Area

19/12/2003 Agreement between the European Union and the Republic of Iceland and the Kingdom of Norway on the application of certain provisions of the Convention of 29 May 2000 on Mutual Assistance in Criminal Matters between the Member States of the European Union and the 2001 Protocol thereto

19/12/2002 Agreement between the European Union and the Kingdom of Norway concerning the participation of the Kingdom of Norway to the European Union Police Mission (EUPM) in Bosnia and Herzegovina

19/01/2001 Agreement between the European Community and the Republic of Iceland and the Kingdom of Norway concerning the criteria and mechanisms for establishing the State responsible for examining a request for asylum lodged in a Member State or in Iceland or Norway - Declarations

19/10/2000 Agreement between the European Community and the Kingdom of Norway on the participation of Norway in the work of the European Monitoring Centre for Drugs and Drug Addition

18/05/1999 Agreement concluded by the Council of the European Union, the Republic of Iceland and the Kingdom of Norway on the association of these two states to the implementation, to application and to the development of the *acquis* de Schengen - final Act

10/04/1997 Agreement on customs cooperation in the form of an Exchange of Letters between the European Community and the Kingdom of Norway

20/12/1995 Agreement in the form of exchange of letters between the kingdom of Norway and the European Community pertaining to certain products of agriculture.

Source: European External Action Service Treaties Office Database.

Index

Page references for notes are followed by n